FOSTORIA

Designer George Sakier

With Values

Leslie Piña

Schiffer Publishing Ltd

77 Lower Valley Road, Atglen, PA 19310

.....*For George, though we never met.*

Library of Congress Cataloging in Publication Data

Fostoria: the designs of George Sakier: with values / Leslie Piña.
p. cm.--(A Schiffer book for collectors)
Includes bibliographical references and index.
ISBN 0-88740-858-3 (hardcover)
1. Sakier, George, 1897-1988--Catalogs.
2. Fostoria Glass Company--Catalogs.
I. Title. II. Series.
NK5198.S23A4 1996
748.2913--dc20 95-37083
CIP

Printed in Hong Kong
ISBN: 0-88740-858-3
We are interested in hearing from authors with book ideas on related topics.

Published by Schiffer Publishing Ltd.
77 Lower Valley Road
Atglen, PA 19310
Please write for a free catalog.
This book may be purchased from the publisher.
Please include $2.95 postage.
Try your bookstore first.

Contents

Credits

While visiting the Huntington Museum of Art to photograph glass for a book on Fostoria, head curator Eason Eige generously opened the "vault" for me and my teenage son Ravi (the photographer who has since retired). I remember Eason's enthusiasm for the Sakier pieces, a name I was only hearing for the first time. In fact, attempts to enlighten me came very near to casting the proverbial pearls before swine — at the time, my experience with American glass was minimal. I did, however, recognize that Eason was a man with a real sense for design and uncommon taste, so I followed his lead in selecting objects to photograph.

Months later, Mitch Attenson of Attenson's Antiques in Cleveland, also with an eye for good design, pointed out a Fostoria Art Deco vase and mentioned something about the Mapplethorpe sale at Christie's. That got my attention, and when I read the name George Sakier in the caption under the auction catalog photograph, I remembered the Huntington pieces.

Shortly after, while at the Dalzell-Viking Glass Co. in New Martinsville, West Virginia, seeking material for a book on West Virginia glass, I mentioned Sakier to the company president Kenneth Dalzell, who also happened to have been the last president of Fostoria Glass. He introduced me to former Fostoria design department head Jon Saffell, and later Mrs. Dalzell (Georgia) sent me an invitation to Sakier's upcoming exhibits in the Pratt Galleries in Manhattan and Brooklyn. That, of course, was the key puzzle piece. In addition to those already mentioned, I would like to thank Pratt Exhibitions Director Eleanor Moretta for helping me to get this project started...and finished. With her introduction, the George Sakier Foundation kindly opened boxes of papers for me and my student and friend Hillary Stone (who also spent many hours searching for patent drawings). Special thanks to Dr. and Mrs. Jacob Israel for access to the material and for their kindness and hospitality. Thanks to Condé Nast Publications Inc. for permission to reprint the photos from *Vogue* and *House and Garden*, to Christie's New York, Sotheby's New York, to Marc Bernier at Pratt for taking photos of archival material, and to Ramón for building photography set-ups and helping to take most of the glass pictures (Ravi took the ones at the Huntington).

I am grateful to many others, such as Dr. Barry Harwood at the Brooklyn Museum, Bill Litman, Jerry Gallagher, Gary Schneider, Glenn and Betty Close, Grace Wilson, and numerous library staffs, especially at the Corning Museum of Glass, Cleveland Public Library, and Ursuline College. Without the help of these people, the serendipitous chain of events, the material at the George Sakier Foundation, and the trust and support of Nancy and Peter Schiffer of Schiffer Publishing (because none of us really knew where this was going), this book would not have been possible. Thank you all.

Sakier in his studio, 1940s. *Courtesy of the George Sakier Foundation.*

Preface

The title *Fostoria Designer: George Sakier* is only partly correct. Sakier was also an important American industrial designer, an interior designer, a graphic designer and art director, and a fine artist who painted in oils. With such versatility, perhaps the title "Designer: George Sakier" would have been more accurate. However, it is the Fostoria glass that he is known for. People do not collect bath fixtures, but they do collect stemware and candleholders, and there is something very appealing about being able to collect the work of a particular artist or designer. Sakier sent his designs to Moundsville, West Virginia, from New York or from Paris for more than half a century. A style he called modern classic added a level of sophistication to a company whose standards of quality were already high. Fostoria's leadership knew a good thing, and Sakier continued to send designs (some little more than, according to Fostoria's last president Kenneth Dalzell, "squiggles on a tissue") until Fostoria fired up its last furnace in 1986. Sakier died in 1988 in Paris.

In today's world of specializations, a multi-faceted talent like Sakier's is exceptional; that he lived and worked so recently is a bit surprising. What is really curious is that his name is not better known. Some designers are so well known that their names are associated with styles and periods and have become familiar, even household words. This notoriety is undoubtedly based on merit. Yet there are other, lesser known, figures whose contributions may have equalled or even exceeded those of the stars. They have yet to be discovered or rediscovered and must be brought to the attention of those who curate exhibits, write, teach, or collect (in addition to following trends, collectors have begun to lead them).

One such name is that of George Sakier, who was on the way to fame along with his esteemed colleagues, some of whom were co-founders of the Society of Industrial Designers (SID). Besides their obvious value to American industrial design, there were often other factors that contributed to the popularity of these designers. For example, Russel Wright launched well-organized publicity campaigns until the department stores recognized his marketing value and began to run full-page newspaper advertisements in which Wright's name overshadowed even that of the retailer. George Nelson, one of this century's most significant designers of furniture and other items, was also an insightful and prolific writer. Nelson's philosophy became as well-known as his designs, thus contributing to his continued recognition. Industrial designers Raymond Loewy, Joseph Sinel, Walter Dorwin Teague, John Vassos, and others also wrote books.

Consistent visibility through exhibits has been another vehicle by which designers have achieved recognition. Viktor Schreckengost, another versatile industrial designer, is also an accomplished ceramic artist. His exposure in the Everson Museum of Art's Ceramic Nationals and the Cleveland Museum of Art's May Shows, for example, have helped to bring his name to the forefront of American design. There are many others whose work has been well recognized and publicized. There are also those designers who have, for one reason or another, been overlooked, or, as in the case of Sakier, forgotten.

Sakier's design career began in the 1920s and took off in the 1930s, as evidenced by contemporary magazine articles and exhibits at museums and the

1939 World's Fair. By about 1950 something unusual happened: he dropped out of sight. Or, more accurately, he joined the ranks of other expatriot artists who left for Europe and remained there for the duration. For unknown reasons, Sakier gave up industrial design, chose to concentrate on painting, and went to Paris. However, he was practical enough and fortunate to be able to keep his ties to the Fostoria Glass Co. in Moundsville, West Virginia. Although he continued to send Fostoria glass designs almost until he died, his career as one of America's pioneer industrial designers was cut short. Yet the decades in which he did kitchen and bath designs were particularly significant, because they were precisely the years in which Modernism in the industrial and decorative arts had its foundations. Sakier's most notable glass designs contributed to that phase of Modernism called Art Deco, and they continued to evolve through the 1950s and later. He may not have remained in the United States long enough to be properly promoted, but Sakier's work in both glass and industrial design was important enough to warrant his inclusion in that loosely defined multidisciplinary group called American Modernists.

Exhibit of Sakier's Fostoria designs. *Courtesy of the George Sakier Foundation.*

Sakier in his studio. *Courtesy of the George Sakier Foundation.*

Chapter One: George Sakier

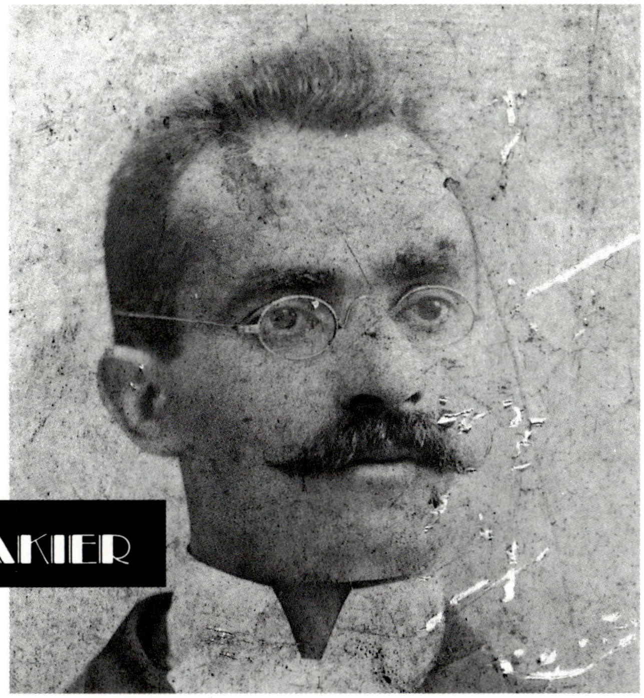

1.1Sakier's father Samuel in Burlington, Vermont, 1894. *Courtesy of the George Sakier Foundation.*

George Sakier kept several versions of his résumé on hand. The items were either roughly chronological or simply by categories. Although the dates are not always consistent, the following compilation of these lists, together with information from other sources listed in the bibliography, should provide a sense of his varied experiences and accomplishments.

Born in New York City, December 23, 1897.
Father, Samuel.
Mother, Sophie.
Brother, Abraham.
Sister, Helen.
Died August 24, 1988 in Paris.

EDUCATION
Pratt Institute, Brooklyn.
Art Students League, New York City.
Columbia University.[1]
Offered a post-graduate scholarship in Physics Dept. at Columbia but did not have the required academic credits.
Brooklyn Polytechnic.
Studied painting in Paris in the early 1920s.

TEACHING
1917-1918, laboratory aid in experiments to Physics Dept. at Columbia.
1918-1920, organized New York City Y. M. C. A School of Machine Design for veterans.
Taught trigonometry and perspective.
Lecture course in Materials at New York University.
Late 1930s, member of the Advisory Council of the Laboratory School of Industrial Design, New York.
Invited by Cooper Union in New York to head their Industrial Design Department.

1.2 Young George Sakier (right) with older brother Abraham and younger sister Helen. Handwritten on reverse, "With compliments to Mrs. F. Rose from Sakier." *Courtesy of the George Sakier Foundation.*

1.3 Sakier's mother Sophie in Burlington, Vermont, 1894. *Courtesy of the George Sakier Foundation.*

1.4 Sakier (left) at age eleven with older brother Abraham and sister Helen. Handwritten on reverse, "With compliments to our beloved aunt — from Abraham, George, and Helen 26/4/09. *Courtesy of the George Sakier Foundation.*

ENGINEERING

1916-1917, draftsman for Lighting Division of Franklin Railway Supply Co.

Invented a pole changer for Franklin's train lighting generator.[2]

Inventions made during this period were later used by the New York Central, B. & O., and other railroads.

MILITARY

1917, trained in United States Army Artillery Camouflage while at Columbia University.

Joined the camouflage corps during World War I; painted camouflage patterns.

1940 in United States Army; appointed Chief Materials Engineer for the War Department.

Developed the first carbon heat exchanger to replace the copper, and was awarded a diploma by the War Manpower Commission Committee for Scientific Research, dated December 15, 1943.

Reserve member as scientific personnel of U.S. War Manpower Commission.

ART DIRECTOR

(exact dates are uncertain since no two sources seem to agree)

1925-1926, assistant art director French *Vogue.*

1926-1927, art director *Modes and Manners.*

1927-1929, art director *Harper's Bazaar*[3]

1920s, Harold Loeb's magazine, *Broom*

INTERIOR DESIGN

Au Quatrième of John Wanamaker's - murals and interiors about 1920.

Bathrooms at World's Fairs.

Furniture designed for specific interiors.

ARCHITECTURE

Designed two houses in Bridgehampton, Long Island.

Designed and built house at 340 E. 71st Street in New York City.

Designed home in Vaucluse, France.

Designed a New York City office building.

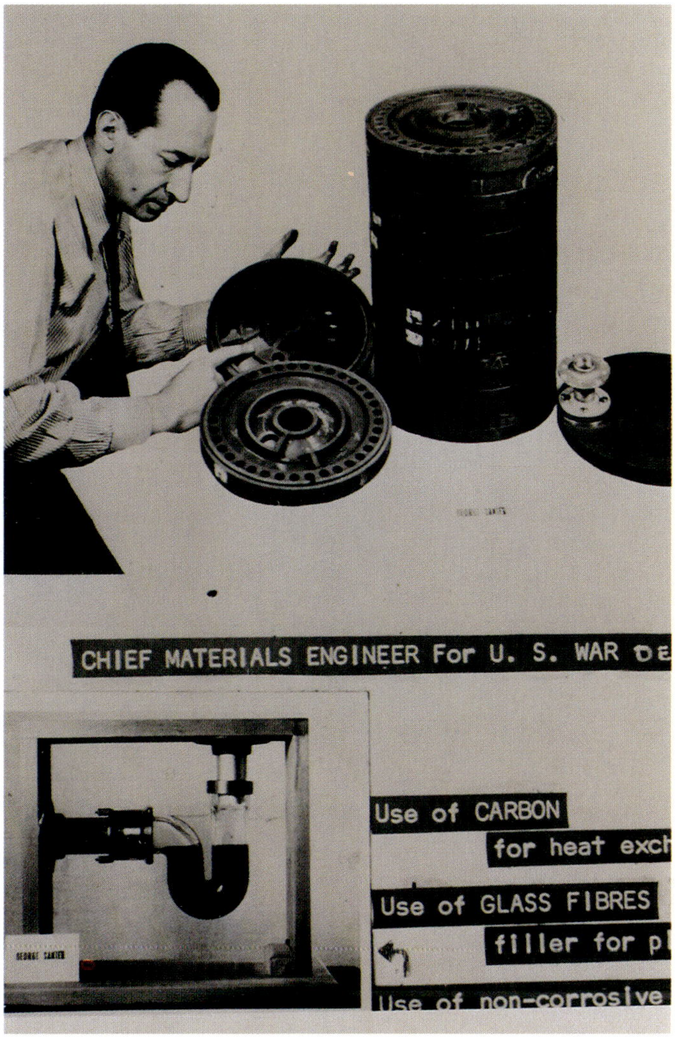

1.5 Sakier as Chief Materials Engineer for the United States War Department, and carbon heat exchanger, early 1940s. *Courtesy of the George Sakier Foundation.*

1.6 Museum exhibit of Sakier designs with carbon heat exchanger in front of shelves of Fostoria glass. *Photo by Karger-Pix, New York, courtesy of the George Sakier Foundation.*

INDUSTRIAL DESIGN

Head of the Bureau of Design at the American Radiator Standard Sanitary Corporation from 1927 to the 1940s, and therefore one of the first in-house full time industrial designers.

Designed the Neo-Classic bathroom fixtures that won the contract for the new Waldorf Astoria hotel in 1931.

Designed the Arco Panel lavatory for the Accessories Company, a division of American Radiator and Standard Sanitary; this was the first prefabricated bathroom, which was installed in the first prefabricated house in 1933.

Charter member of Society of Industrial Designers in 1944.

Designed for Sauter and for Forges de Strasbourg in France.

Designed Unitube oil paint tube holder and palette.

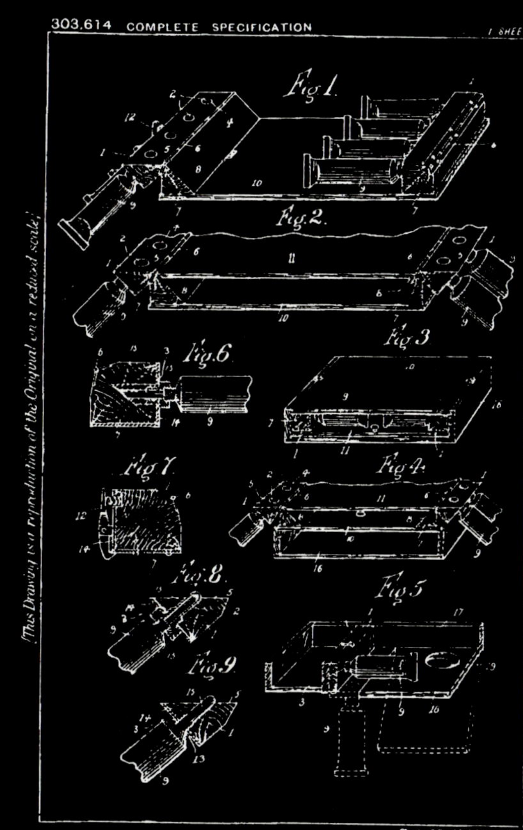

1.7 Drawing for a device for holding and storing tubes of artist's colors and for releasing the paint, while also serving as a palette. British patent applied for on Nov. 17, 1927, and received Jan. 10, 1929.

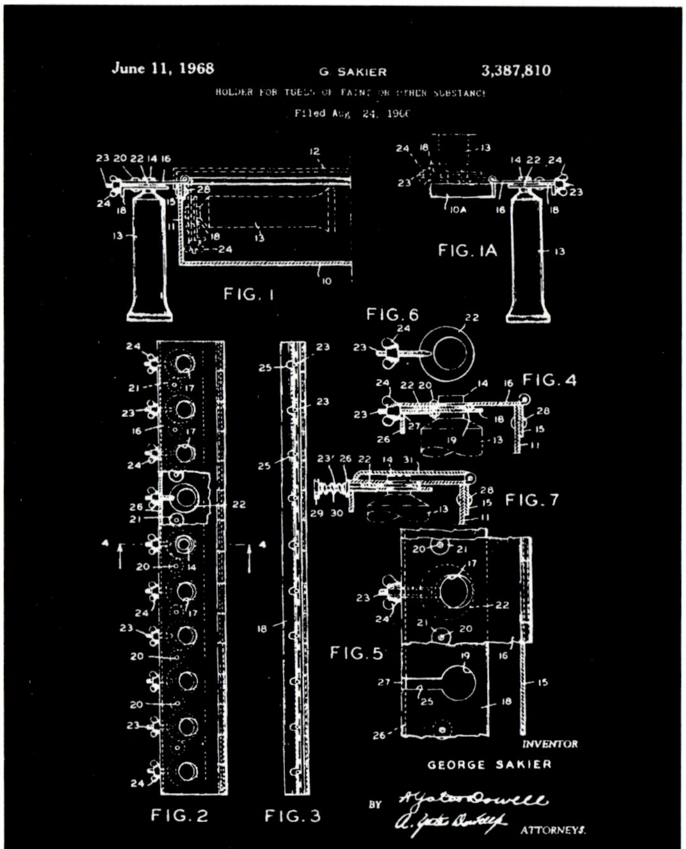

1.8 Drawing for paint tube holder and palette. American patent applied for Aug. 24, 1966 and received June 11, 1968.

1.9 Sakier's "Unitube" palette with patents held in the United States and Great Britain (illustrated) plus France and Germany. *Courtesy of the George Sakier Foundation.*

1.10 Sakier using his Unitube palette. *Courtesy of the George Sakier Foundation.*

GLASS AND CERAMIC DESIGN

1929-1979+ Fostoria Glass Co. main consultant (outside) designer; responsible for most of the company's Art Deco and other high style modern designs.

Venini & Co. of Murano, Italy - glass designs.

American Goldscheider and possibly also Goldscheider of Vienna, Austria - ceramic designs.

L. F. Grammes & Sons, Allentown, Pennsylvania - ceramic designs.

Animal Trap Company of America, Lititz, Pennsylvania - ceramic designs.

PACKAGING DESIGN

Schenley Liquor's leading brand, Old Schenley, which was reinstated after prohibition: designed bottles, labels, wrappers, cartons, and promotional literature.

Alfred Dunhill: "Men's Toiletries" packaging.

Dunhill women's perfume "Escape" packaging.

1.11 Ceramic designs shown in article "George Sakier: Artist and Machine Become Reconciled." Caption reads, "Majolica glazed ceramics in white and azure blue — American Goldscheider Co." *Courtesy of the George Sakier Foundation.*

1.12 Majolica vase by American Goldscheider Co. also illustrated in magazine article. *Courtesy of the George Sakier Foundation.*

EXHIBIT DESIGN

Designed five exhibits at 1933 Chicago World's Fair.

Designed two of the seven theme exhibits, Science and Education, at the 1939 New York World's Fair.

EXHIBITS OF GLASS AND PAINTING

New York World's Fair - glass.

San Francisco Golden Gate World's Fair - glass.

Chicago Century of Progress Exhibition.

Pennsylvania Museum of Art.

Philadelphia Museum of Art - glass.

Philadelphia Art Alliance - one man show, painting, 1949.

Metropolitan Museum of Art - glass.

Brooklyn Museum - glass.

Museum of Modern Art "Machine Art" exhibit - glass, 1934.

Whitney Museum of American Art - glass, 1985.

Yale Art Museum - glass.

Worcester Museum, Worcester, Massachusetts - glass.

Guild Hall, East Hampton, New York - painting.

Parish Art Museum, Southampton, New York - painting, 1970.

Benson Gallery, Bridgehampton, New York - painting.

Byron Gallery, New York City - painting.

Galerie Julien Lévy, Paris - painting, 1918.

Julien Levy Gallery, New York City - painting, 1960.

Musée des Arts Décoratifs, the Louvre, Paris - glass.

Galerie Jacques Massol, Paris - painting, 1963.

Galerie Denise René, Paris - painting, 1960s.

Galerie St. Andre des Arts, Paris - painting.

Premiere Exposition des Galeries Pilotes, Lausanne, Switzerland - painting, 1960s.

Musée des Beaux-Arts, Lausanne, Switzerland - painting.

O'Hana Gallery, London - painting.

Mona Bismarck Foundation exhibit in Paris - painting, 1987.

Pratt Manhattan Gallery - painting and glass, 1994.

1.13 Sakier designs of vase and bowls for the noted Venini glass factory of Italy. *Courtesy of the George Sakier Foundation.*

1.14 Sakier's candleholder design for Venini. *Courtesy of the George Sakier Foundation.*

Schafler Gallery (Pratt), Brooklyn - painting and glass, 1994.

AWARDS

1932, National Alliance of Art & Industry Award for Fostoria glass design.

1935, American Management Association national award.

1937, *Studio Yearbook* awards.

1939, Schenley Products logo award for Old Schenley Liquor.

1943, National Cosmetics Industry Award for Alfred Dunhill package.

1943, Packaging Award of Beauty Fashion Magazine for Mary Dunhill "Escape" package.

1.15 Sakier's table centerpiece design for Venini. *Courtesy of the George Sakier Foundation.*

1.16 Two-tiered table centerpiece design for Venini. *Courtesy of the George Sakier Foundation.*

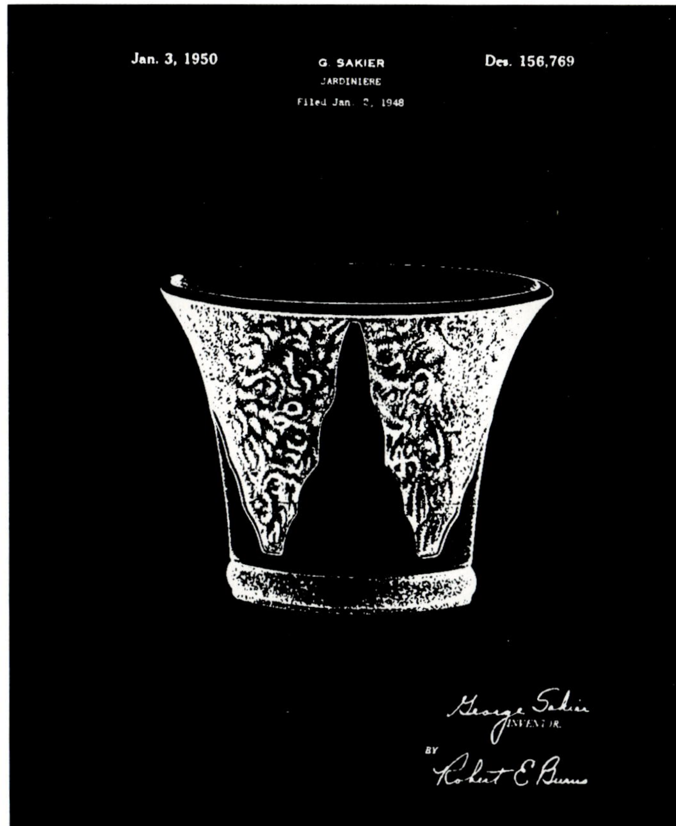

1.17 Patent drawing of pottery jardiniere for the Animal Trap Company of America in Lititz, Pennsylvania, applied for Jan. 2, 1948 and issued Jan. 3, 1950.

PUBLICATIONS

Machine Design and Descriptive Geometry, 1913.

Manuals on trigonometry and perspective.

Article on Mayan art in the 1920s; influenced the Trocadero Museum to display their important collection of Pre-Columbian art.

Articles in *Fortune*

House & Garden

Architectural Forum

Pottery and Glass Journal

Arts and Decoration

The Broom

l'Amour de l'Art.

PAINTING

1922-24, went to Europe on a freighter; traveled, painted, and supported himself by writing articles on American engineering for European publications and articles on European art for American publications.

Continued to paint while in Paris in mid 1920s.

Couples painted in 1926.

Friends included Hans Arp, Marcel Duchamp, Max Ernst, Willem de Kooning, Isamu Noguchi, Man Ray, Mark Rothko, Rufino Tamayo, and Sophie Tauber.

1950 relocated to Paris to devote full time to painting.

Studios at 44 rue du Bac, Paris; New York City; Bridgehampton, Long Island.

1.18 Sculptor/ designer Isamu Noguchi in Sakier's apartment. Handwritten on reverse, "Noguchi and our cats." *Courtesy of the George Sakier Foundation.*

1.19 Painting from the Abstract Couple series used as the cover illustration of the exhibition announcement for "George Sakier: Correspondences" held at Pratt Institute in New York in 1994, oil on canvas, 28 3/4 by 29 in. *Courtesy of Pratt and the George Sakier Foundation.*

1.20 Collage from the Abstract Landscape series used to illustrate the inside of the exhibit announcement, oil on paper collage, 12 3/8 by 11 1/2 in. *Courtesy of Pratt and the George Sakier Foundation.*

Chapter Two: Fostoria Glass Design

The Fostoria Glass Company is not usually thought of as a source of modern design, original or otherwise. Its first factory opened in 1887 in the northwestern Ohio town of Fostoria, because a factory site and supply of natural gas were offered at no charge. Like other nineteenth-century American glass manufacturers, Fostoria produced Victorian pressed pattern glass. This colorless tableware was of a high quality and firepolished to give a bright finish. They also made fruit jars and a variety of oil lamps in the same patterns as the tableware.

Above: 2.1 Ebony square-footed tumblers, line 4020, with gold rings on crystal bowl, decoration 604 Club Design B. *Photo by Nickolas Murray, courtesy of the George Sakier Foundation.*

Left: 2.2 Number 4020 decanter with square foot and footed tumbler with 703 New Yorker cutting. The photograph appeared in the "Designer & Industry" Exhibition of the National Alliance of Art & Industry at 65 E. 56th St. in New York City, *Decorators Digest* in 1933, and *Studio Yearbook* in 1935. *Courtesy of the George Sakier Foundation.*

When the gas supply proved to be unreliable, the factory relocated in Moundsville, West Virginia and reopened on the first day of 1892. They continued to make the same kinds of items until the 1920s when William Alexander Baxter Dalzell, who had become president of the company in 1902, began a series of innovations and improvements. Colored tableware was introduced in 1924, followed by the first complete glass dinnerware sets in 1925. At the same time, they began a national advertising campaign and created a design department. Calvin B. Roe, Dalzell's right hand man and vice president, became president in 1928 after Dalzell died. In 1945 Roe was succeeded by Dalzell's son, William F. Dalzell, who had worked for the company since 1915. His son, David Beaty Dalzell, became president in 1968, followed by his son, Kenneth B. Dalzell in 1982.

It would be interesting to know how Sakier, an East Coast modernist painter, engineer, and industrial designer came to design glassware for Middle America. His relationship with Fostoria proved to be perfectly symbiotic: both won acclaim for design excellence, and both reaped monetary rewards. One author, writing in 1935, described Sakier's glass designs for moderately-priced tableware as "part of the widespread industrial design activity which is introducing a modern art standard to commodities hitherto without appearance standards."[1] Whether the implication was that Fostoria lacked appearance standards in general or just lacked pre-Sakier modernism is not important. There was also a strong American market for traditional patterns, as evidenced by the company's illustrated catalogs and increasing sales. What Sakier introduced was a level of sophistication that carried Fostoria into an international arena.

It was the modern work that proved newsworthy. Contemporary journalists made remarks about Sakier and his designs such as, "American openstock glass for the first time took precedence over European, and he won the distinction of having his own designs for glass pirated in Europe."[2] Sakier was described as "one of the first American designers whose work was copied abroad."[3] His widely admired square-based tumblers, line 4020, were declared to be "responsible for the disintegration of the European glass monopoly in America," and before that design was introduced, "none in this country could compare with imported examples from the standpoint of design compatible with price."[4]

Although Sakier had secured a design patent, the square foot with short corkscrew stem was quickly copied in America as well. Fenton introduced their number 1639 two-toned and nearly identical tumbler in 1931; Heisey used a square foot as well as square plates and saucers for their New Era pattern in 1934;

2.3 Copy of Sakier's 4020 design made by Fenton in 1931, number 1639 footed wine in ebony with alabaster white square foot.

Cambridge used the square foot and a square-centered round plate in 1949. A rather puzzling copy, was made right at Fostoria. When resident designer Edgar Bottome designed the New Garland etching, he used Sakier's stemware design to display it. Bottome apparently added some height to the corkscrew stem and patented, or repatented Sakier's design in 1931. It is not only odd, but awkward to attribute the line to Sakier and also give credit to Bottome for extending the height of the stem of some pieces. Yet that seems to be what happened.

There were other original American Art Deco glass designs besides Sakier's Fostoria: Consolidated Lamp & Glass Co. in Corapolis, Pennsylvania, introduced a very modern line of tableware called Ruba Rombic in 1928; Phoenix Glass Co. introduced modern designs in the 1930s; Libbey Glass Co. had their Syncopation cocktail glasses in 1933 and number 4900 Embassy designed by Edwin W. Fuerst and Walter Dorwin Teague in 1939. Teague's modern designs were also produced by Steuben Glass Works in the 1930s. Other Steuben designers at the time included the earlier master of color and Art Nouveau, Frederick Carder, and Sidney Waugh. But Steuben, unlike Fostoria, produced art glass for the high end of the market.

Sakier was an industrial designer committed to both modernism and mass production, and his glass designs were intended to express both. Another of his designs that has also received more recent attention is a fluted vase, line 2428 Lotus vase. In the Whitney Museum exhibition catalog *High Styles*, the vase is compared to "the geometricized and abstracted classicism of the Wiener Werkstätte," which was introduced by Austrian-born modernist Paul Frankl and Austrian emigres such as Joseph Urban.[5] I think Sakier would have liked that. In fact, a table he designed for his East 57th Street New York apartment looked remarkably similar to a table and chairs in Urban's office reception room.[6]

No doubt, Sakier had an identifiable style. Yet, until more documentation is found, it will be difficult to estimate the number of glass designs that can be attributed to him. His first designs for Fostoria were from 1929, but it would not be surprising to learn that a few preceded that date. In a letter to Sakier dated March 22, 1979, Fostoria president David B. Dalzell recognized him for having been with the company for fifty years, and, yes, he had a gold watch to present to him. More importantly, he wrote, "Your record of design success with us will probably never be equalled because of the many years with the company and the volume of sales generated." He added, "for those of us who

2.4 Table designed by Sakier with strong Wiener Werkstätte influence. *Courtesy of the George Sakier Foundation.*

have had the pleasure of working with you, it [the watch] has a more special meaning and an opportunity to try to express our respect for you as a person as well as your ability."[7]

Some time after Sakier's best years at Fostoria — the 1930s and 1940s — the company gradually slipped back into a safer traditionalism. In another letter, this one handwritten and dated March 22, 1981, Dalzell spoke of design meetings they had been having. He wrote, "how I wish we had someone like you to help us. Going through our old catalogs, we can spot a 'Sakier piece;' they are truly good, George. We have no one with your spark or originality, and it is needed now more than ever." He went on to talk about the family. Patty and Michael had a permanent home in London, so he spoke of visiting Sakier in Paris. "Seeing you has always been one of my treasured pleasures in life," and he signed the letter, "With affection."[8] Dalzell could spot a "Sakier piece" because each one possessed an elegant modernity, a simplicity of line and form that did stand out from other designs.

2.5 Number 2428 Lotus vases designed in 1929. This photograph was used to illustrate mass produced glassware in Cheney, *Art and the Machine* p. 221. *Courtesy of the George Sakier Foundation.*

The other designs of Fostoria's last decades could only be described as conservative and bland, and Dalzell's disappointment comes as no surprise. He may not have known the exact year, but it is likely that Dalzell anticipated the sale of the company to Lancaster Colony and later, its final closing in 1986. In retrospect, Fostoria will be remembered as a great company in the history of American glassmaking. With his high style modernism, George Sakier gave Fostoria its day in the sun in the history of glass design.

2.6 Top, 2428 Lotus vase introduced in 1928; bottom, 2430 Diadem 8-in. vase with 702 Comet cutting also 1929. *Courtesy of the George Sakier Foundation.*

2.7 Diadem 2430 in ebony with crystal base, 11-in. bowl and 8-in. vases, 1929-44. *Courtesy of the George Sakier Foundation.*

2.8 Diadem vases in ebony, h. 3 3/4 in; h. 5 3/4 in with cover; and gold tint, h. 6 7/8 in.

2.9 Detail of Diadem base.

2.10 Number 6202 goblet, h. 6 7/8 in., and tumbler, both with amber bowl and crystal foot.

2.11 Companion to Diadem 2430, footed tumblers number 6202 (same as 6002) with diamond pattern above the foot, amber bowl with crystal base, h. 6 in., introduced in 1930.

2.12 Detail of tumbler pattern.

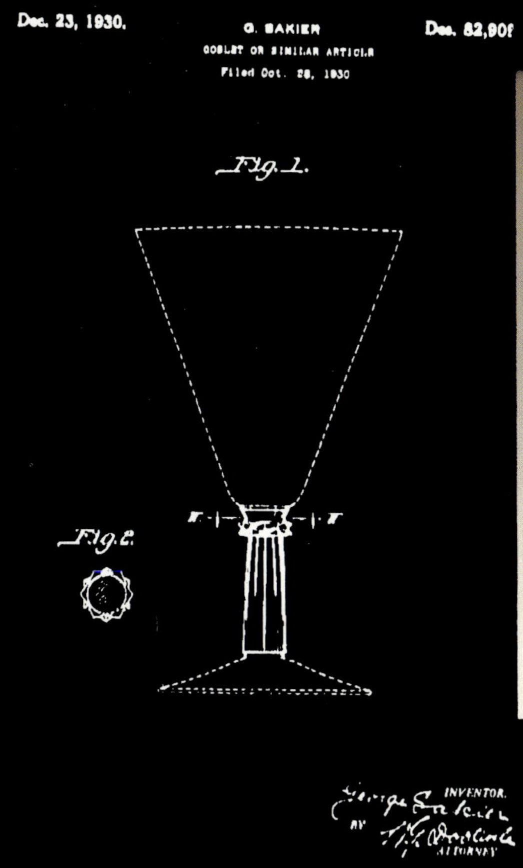

2.13 Detail of goblet stem top.

Above Left: 2.14 Patent drawing for 6202 goblet, filed Oct. 28, 1930, issued Dec. 23, 1930.

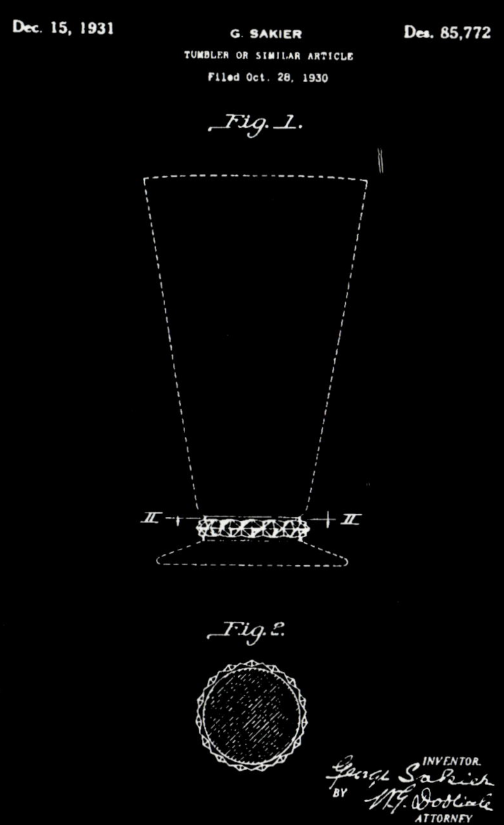

2.15 Patent drawing for 6202 tumbler, filed Oct. 28, 1930, issued Dec. 15, 1931.

2.16 Lotus vase in ebony. *Courtesy of the George Sakier Foundation.*

2.17 Number 2425 rectangular Art Deco vase, pictured in the 1935 *Studio Yearbook*; an ebony example is in the Brooklyn Museum collection. *Courtesy of the George Sakier Foundation.*

2.18 Lot # 62 of the June 10 & 11, 1993 *Twentieth Century Decorative Arts* sale: 2428 Lotus vases in silver mist, crystal, and ebony with 2425 vase. *© Sotheby's Inc. Courtesy of Sotheby's New York.*

2.19 Group of Art Deco vases, lots 106-109 from Christie's Oct. 31, 1989 sale for the benefit of the Robert Mapplethorpe Foundation: top, 2428 Lotus vases in crystal, silver mist, amber, wisteria, and topaz, and 2387 vase in rose; center, 2408 vase in green with 2425 vases in azure, ebony, topaz, and green, and a 2428 vase in rose; bottom, 2404, 2409, and 2428 vases in topaz; front, 2404 in green. *Courtesy Christie's New York.*

2.20 Lotus vases: left, 13-in. in blue; right, 9-in. vase in topaz with silver mist matte finish (made from 1934 to 1940). *Courtesy of the Huntington Museum of Art.*

2.21 Lotus vases in amber (h. 13 in.), green, and azure, 1930. *Courtesy of the Huntington Museum of Art.*

2.22 Art Deco 2409 vase in green, h. 8 in., 1930.

2.23 Art Deco 2409 vase in ebony, h. 8 in., late 1950s, paper label.

2.24 Art Deco 2404 vase in fishbowl shape with concentric circles, h. 5 1/2 in., d. 6 1/2 in., 1930. *Courtesy of the Huntington Museum of Art.*

2.25 Art Deco 2404 vase in gold.

2.26 Number 4101 vase in rose, h. 5 1/4 in., 1929.

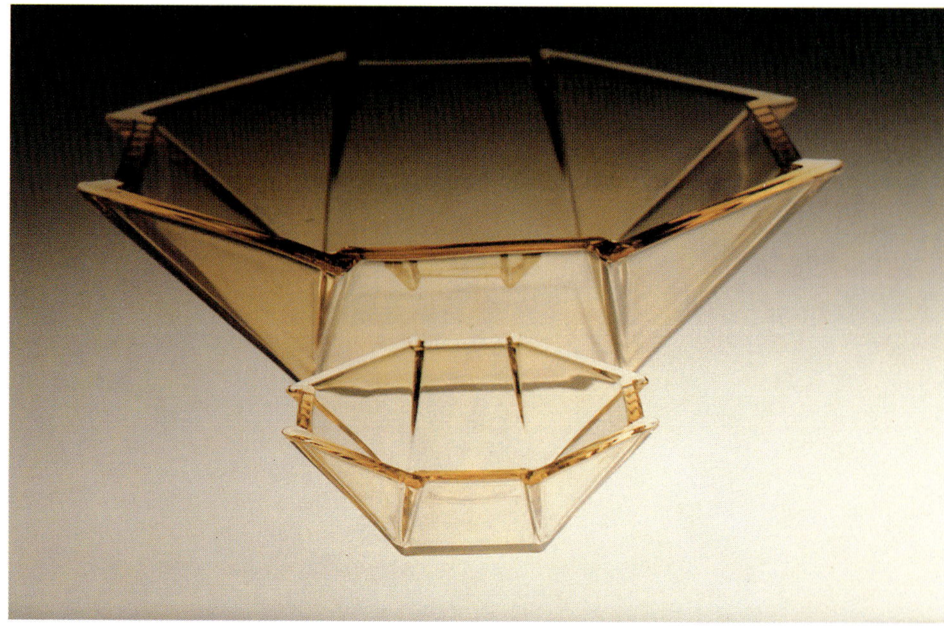

2.27 Number 2402 geometric bowl, h. 3 1/8 in., d. 10 in., with small bowl, h. 1 3/4 in., d. 4 1/8 in., both in gold tint, 1930.

2.28 Different angle of 2402 bowls, together with candleholders, also in gold tint.

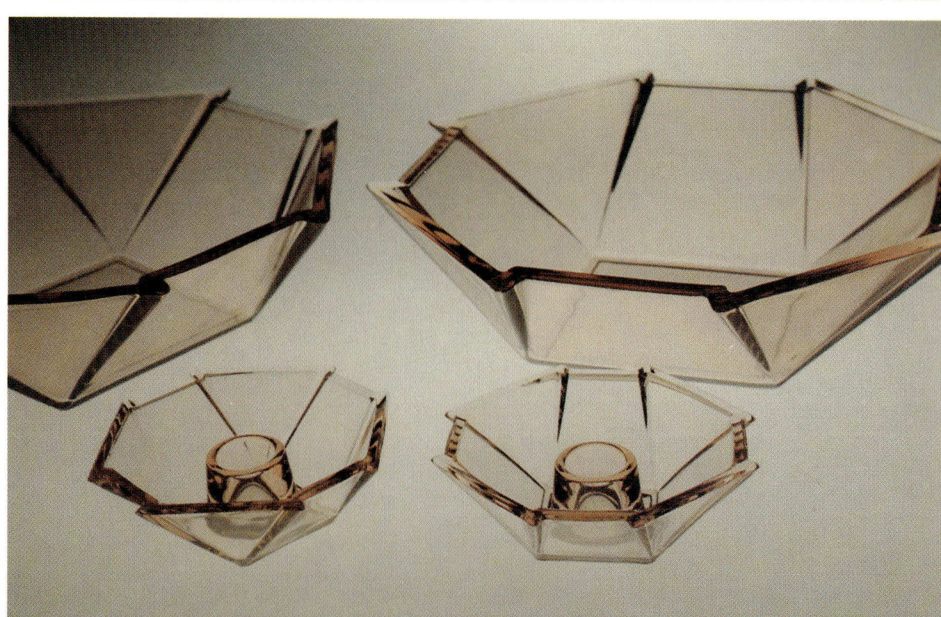

2.29 Number 2402 large 10-in. bowls with 4-in. candleholders in rose.

2.30 Group of 2402 4-in. bowls.

2.31 Medium-sized 8 1/2-in. and small 4-in. bowls.

2.32 Small candleholders in ebony.

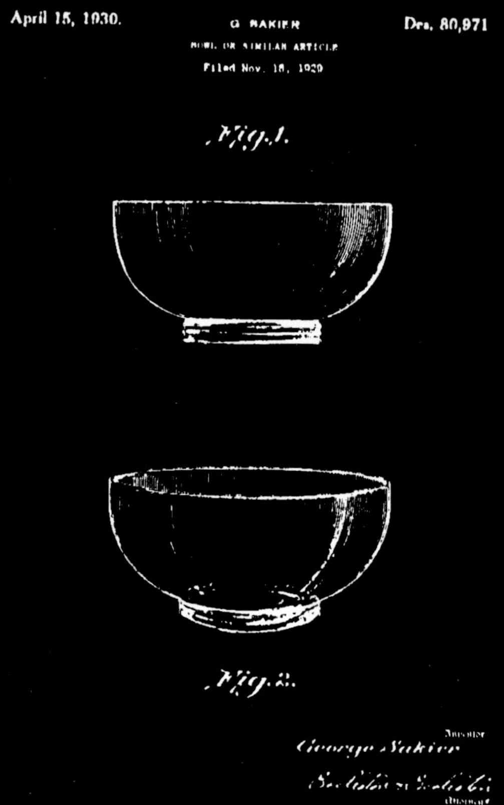

2.33 Patent drawing for 4020 footed finger bowl, filed Nov. 15, 1929, issued April 15, 1930.

2.34 Patent drawing for 4020 low sherbet, filed Nov. 15, 1929, issued April 15, 1930.

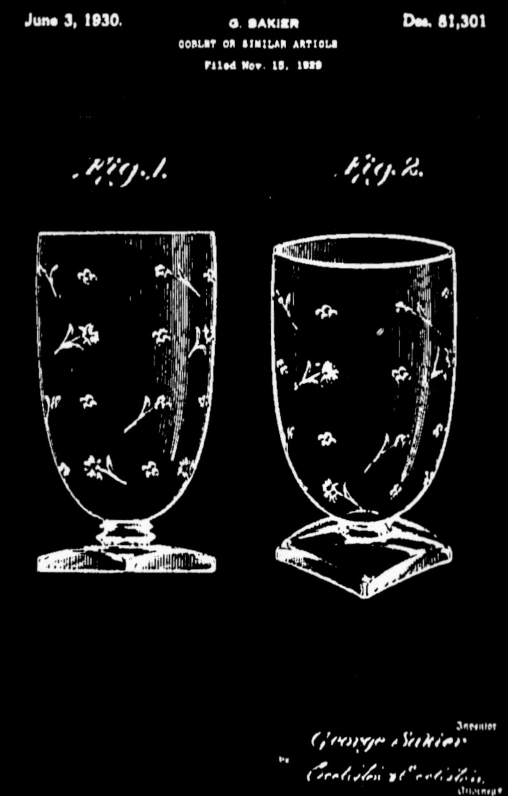

2.35 Patent drawing for 4021 footed tumblers with 195 Millefleur cutting, filed Nov 15, 1929, issued June 3, 1930.

2.36 Patent drawing for 4020 plain footed tumbler, filed Nov. 15, 1929, issued June 3, 1930.

2.37 Left, 4020 footed tumbler with alternating single and double gold bands on crystal, a variant of the 603 Club Design A (normally black bands); center left, low sherbet with gold bands on crystal, 604 Club Design B, with ebony base; center right, goblet with crystal bowl and amber base; right, goblet with Manhattan 725 cutting on crystal bowl and a green base. *Courtesy of the Huntington Museum of Art.*

2.38 Detail of short stem.

2.39 Left, high sherbet with 607 Polka Dot decoration on crystal bowl with ebony base; center, low cocktail with crystal bowl with 700 Formal Garden cutting and ebony base; right, footed tumbler with Formal Garden cutting and ebony base, all 1930-31. *Courtesy of the Huntington Museum of Art.*

2.40 Footed juice with 305 Fern plate etching on crystal bowl with ebony base, h. 4 1/4 in.; with high sherbet with crystal bowl and ebony base, h. 4 1/2 in.

2.41 Detail of Fern etching.

2.42 Goblet with 604 Club Design B, gold gilt bands on crystal bowl, and ebony base, 1929-43. *Courtesy of the Huntington Museum of Art.*

2.43 Footed tumblers with plain crystal bowls and ebony bases, h. 5 1/8 in.

2.44 Low sherbets, all crystal with Comet cutting, h. 3 1/4 in.

2.45 Low sherbets with Comet cutting on crystal bowls and ebony bases.

2.46 Comet cutting on crystal with ebony base: left, tumbler; top center, goblet; bottom center, low cocktail; right, low sherbet. *Courtesy of the Huntington Museum of Art.*

2.47 Footed tumblers with crystal bowls and Comet cutting (one plain) with ebony bases.

2.48 Number 4020 sugar and creamer with Comet cutting on crystal with ebony base, h. 3 1/2 in.

2.49 Queen Anne etching on 4020 crystal tumblers.

2.50 New Garland 284 plate etching on 4020 stems with topaz bowls and crystal bases: goblet h. 5 7/8 in.; footed tumblers h. 5 1/8 and 5 5/8 in.; footed juice h. 4 1/8 in.

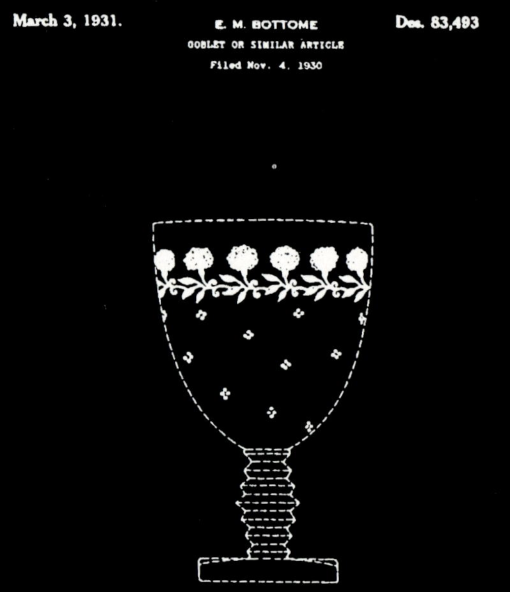

2.51 Patent drawing for New Garland etching, filed by Edgar Bottome on Nov. 4, 1930, and issued Mar. 3, 1931.

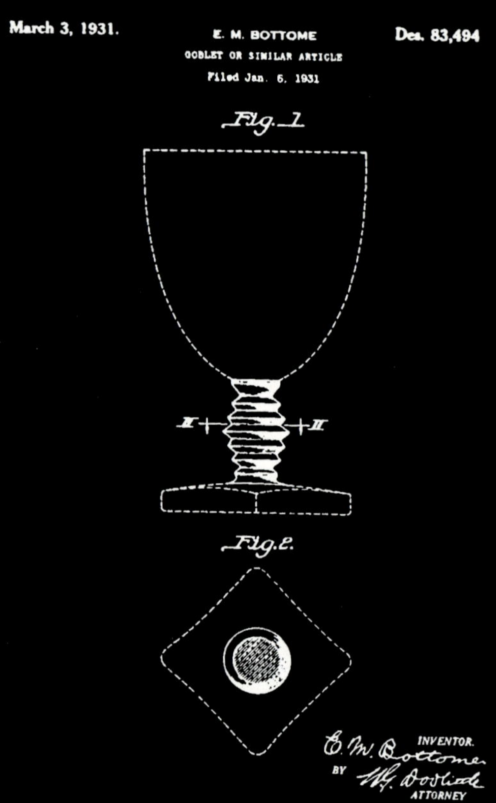

2.52 Patent drawing for Sakier's 4020 design, but filed by Edgar Bottome on Jan. 6, 1931, and issued Mar. 3, 1931. Sakier's original patent was filed in 1929 and issued in 1930, so it is puzzling that Bottome would receive another patent, when the only change is some extended height to the original stem design. It would be more logical to attribute the complete stem line to Sakier and the etching to Bottome.

2.53 New Garland etching on 4020 goblet.

2.54 Goblets and low footed cocktails, h. 2 1/2 in., with wisteria bowls and crystal bases.

2.55 Detail of cocktail.

2.56 Detail of goblet stem.

2.57 Fostoria logo; 4120 (variant of 4020) crystal pitcher with Millefleur 195 cutting on an amber base, 1929-40; and 6045 Capri goblet with crystal bowl on ebony base, h. 5 7/8 in. *Courtesy of the Huntington Museum of Art.*

2.58 Capri claret/wine and sherbet in all crystal, 1952-65.

Above: 2.59 Number 2433 modern classical candlestick with clear bowl and amber base, h. 3 3/4 in., d. 4 7/8 in.; and low compote, h. 3 1/2 in., d. 6 1/8 in. Although the name on the patent (bowl number 85,064 and candle number 85,065 filed Jan. 21, 1931) is E. Stahl, this is a Sakier design and his sketchbooks included several versions of it.

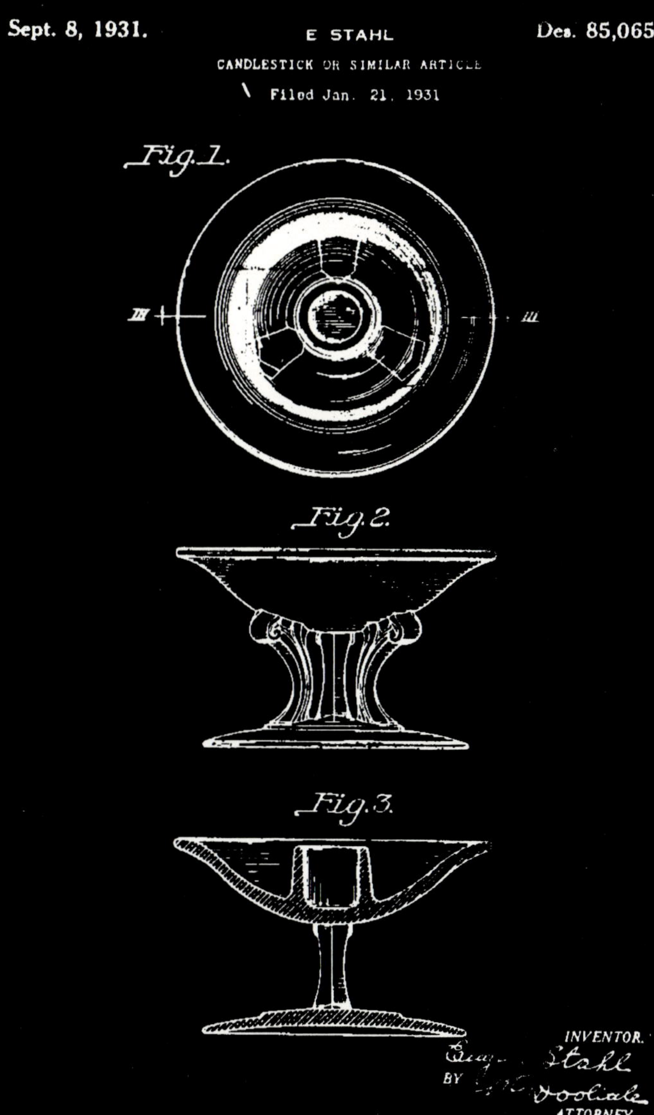

Left: 2.60 Patent drawing for 2433 candlestick, filed Jan. 21, 1931, and issued Sept. 8, 1931.

2.61 Typical Art Deco form, 2419 Mayfair compote in green, h. 5 1/4 in., d. 5 1/2 in.

2.62 Mayfair 7-in. plate with cups and saucers in green, 1930-31, pictured in *Arts and Decoration* in 1935.

2.63 Detail of cup handle.

2.64 Mayfair 10-in. cake plate with handles (actual measurement is 11 1/2 in.) in gold tint, 1938-44.

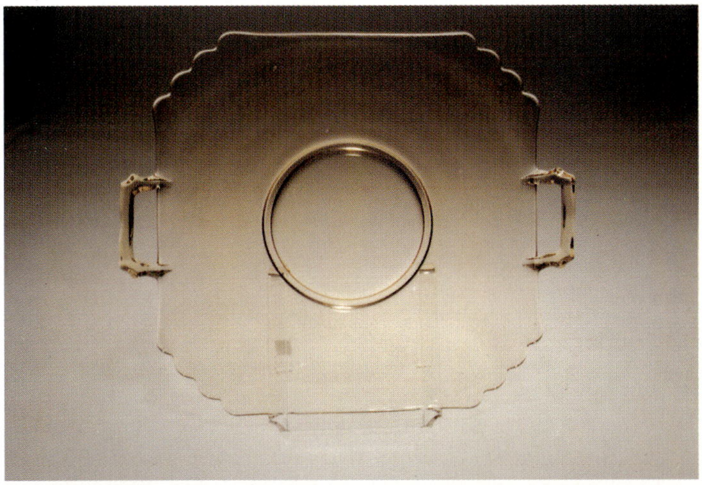

2.66 Mayfair 7-in. plates in ebony, 1930-42.

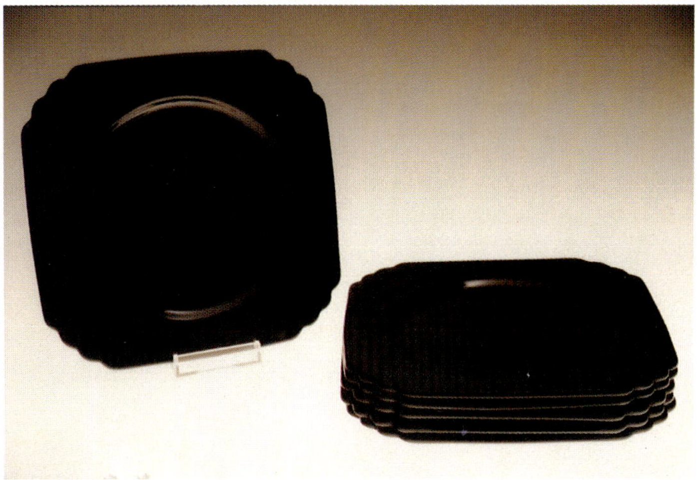

2.65 Stack of Mayfair 7-in. plates in gold tint, or topaz.

2.67 The 2449 Hermitage pattern is said to have been designed by Sakier: goblet, h. 5 1/4 in., with 2449 1/2 shot glass, h. 2 1/2 in., both crystal, 1932-45. *Courtesy of Jerry Gallagher.*

2.68 Hermitage 2449 1/2 old fashioned/cocktails in wisteria, topaz, green, and azure, h. 3 1/4 in., 1932-42. *Courtesy of Jerry Gallagher.*

2.69 Pair of 2447 duo candlesticks (also illustrated in contemporary periodicals) in rose, h. 5 1/8 in., w. 6 5/8 in.

2.70 Pair of 2447 duo candlesticks in green.

2.71 Pair of 2447 duo candlesticks in yellow tint, or topaz.

2.72 Number 2447 circular candlestick. Examples were pictured in 1933 in *Studio Yearbook*, in *Arts and Decoration*, and in *Crockery and Glass Journal*, as well as *U.S. Industrial Design 1949-1950. Courtesy of the George Sakier Foundation.*

2.73 Detail of Sunray candlestick center.

2.74 Pair of 2510 Sunray duo candlesticks, h. 6 1/2 in., w. 7 3/8 in. illustrated in 1935 Fostoria catalog and 1937 *Studio Yearbook*.

2.75 Sunray bowl. Although, so far, only the attribution of the candleholder of this pattern has been documented, it is likely that Sakier was also responsible for the other items.

2.76 Detail of bowl handle.

2.77 Sunray round and three-sided nappies in crystal alternating with yellow.

2.78 Sunray round nappy on handled saucer.

Above: 2.79 2496 Baroque trindle candlesticks in crystal, h. 5 1/2 in., w. 8 1/4 in., 1933-1966.

Left: 2.80 Patent drawing for Baroque trindle candle filed Dec. 19, 1933, and issued Mar. 6, 1934.

Below: 2.81 Detail of single candle.

2.82 2496 Baroque duo candlesticks in crystal, h. 4 1/2 in., w. 8 in., pictured in *Country Life* in 1933.

2.83 Baroque 4-in. single candlesticks in crystal, actual h. 3 7/8 in., w. 4 1/2 in.

2.84 Baroque single candlestick with 329 Lido plate etching.

2.85 Baroque two-light candelabra. These were pictured in 1933 issues of *Arts and Decoration* and *Crockery and Glass Journal* indicating that they were produced before applying for a patent.

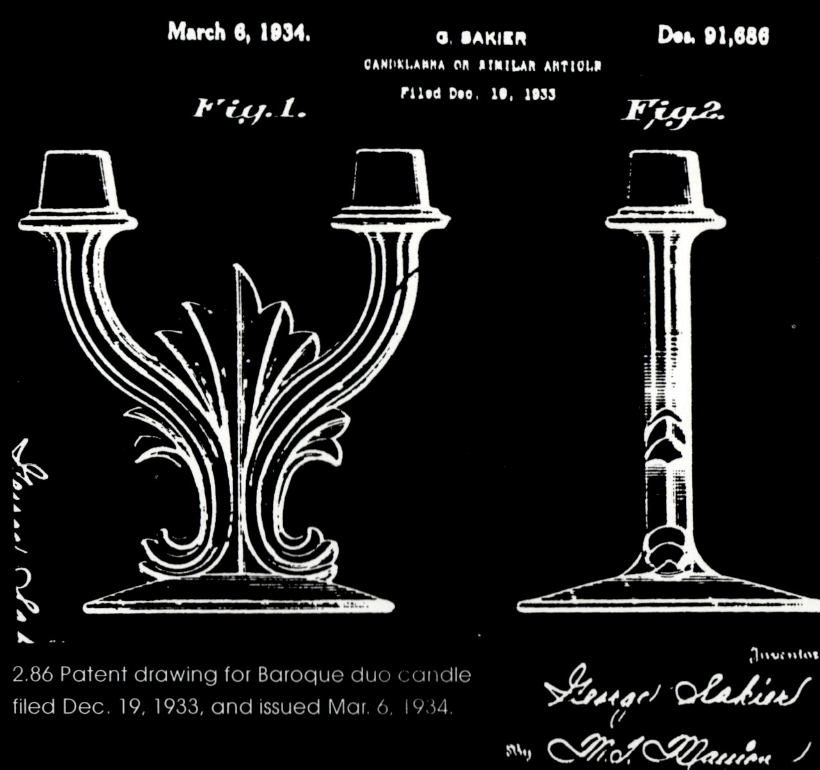

2.86 Patent drawing for Baroque duo candle filed Dec. 19, 1933, and issued Mar. 6, 1934.

2.87 Baroque three-light candelabra, h. 9 in., w. 10 3/4 in.

2.88 Patent drawing for Baroque three-light candelabrum, filed Jan. 2, 1934, and issued Mar. 6, 1934.

2.90 2484 Baroque two and three-light candelabra. *Courtesy of the George Sakier Foundation.*

2.89 Baroque three-light candelabrum.

2.91 2484 Baroque two-light candelabrum, h. 8 1/4 in., w. 10 in. *Photo by Adams Studio, courtesy of the George Sakier Foundation.*

2.92 2496 Baroque single candlesticks in gold tint, h. 5 3/4 in., 1938-44.

2.93 Detail of single candle.

2.94 Baroque single candlesticks in blue, 1936-44. *Courtesy of Jerry Gallagher.*

2.95 Baroque jelly (without cover), h. 5 1/2 in., and compote, h. 4 3/4 in.

2.96 Detail of compote stem.

2.97 2484 Baroque vase, h. 8 in.

2.98 2484 Baroque 10-in. handled bowl, h. 4 1/4 in., l. 15 3/4 in.

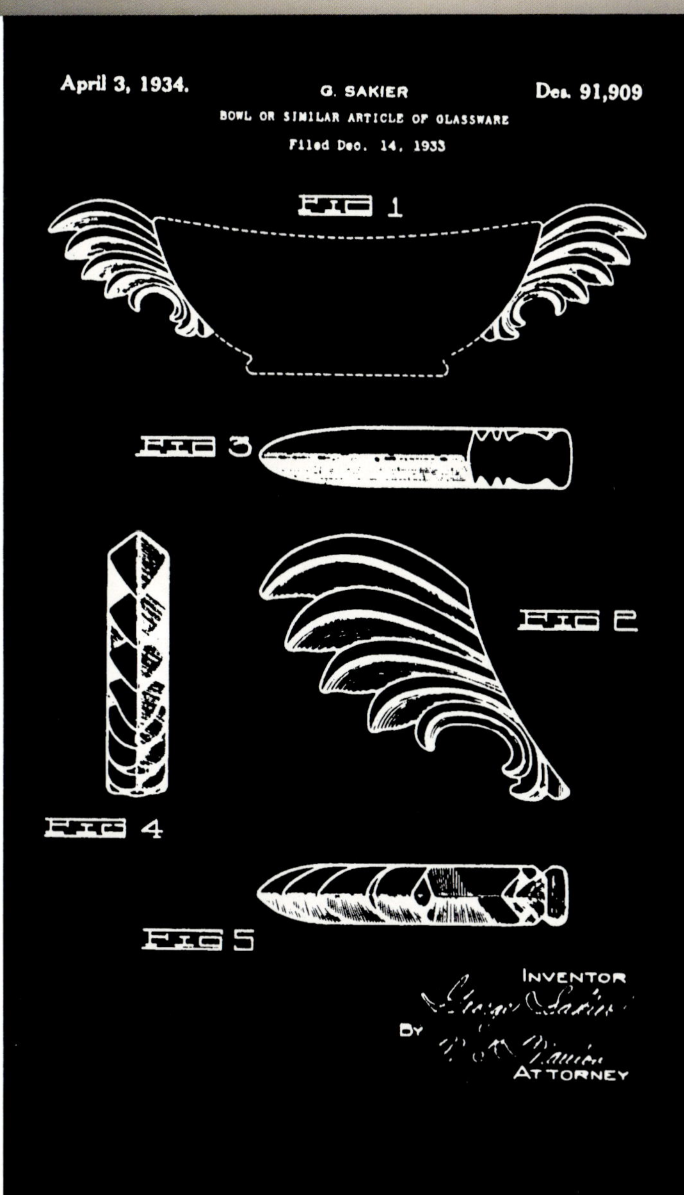

2.99 Detail of bowl handle.

Left: 2.100 Patent drawing for handled bowl, filed Dec. 14, 1933, and issued April 3, 1934.

2.101 2545 Flame handled lunch tray, h. 3 3/4 in., d. 11 1/2 in., mid 1930s-1944.

2.102 Detail of flame.

2.103 Flame duo candlesticks in azure and crystal, h. 6 3/4 in., w. 10 1/4 in. These were pictured in the 1937 *Studio Yearbook.*

2.104 Detail of flame.

2.105 Flame duo with single candlesticks in crystal.

Below Left: 2.106 Flame single candlesticks in blue.

2.108 Flame lustre in crystal, with bobache and prisms added by Fostoria to Sakier's original design, h. 7 1/2 in. *Collection of Grace Wilson.*

2.107 Flame single candlesticks in crystal, h. 4 3/4 in.

2.110 Plain Neo-Classic stems in a contemporary photo, produced 1934-43 plus re- introduction of some items 1949-65. *Courtesy of the George Sakier Foundation.*

2.109 6011 Neo-Classic stemware with 730 Whirlpool cutting, produced 1934-39. This photo appeared in an article, "Contemporary American Glass," in the 1936 *Studio Yearbook*, p. 128, and in a 1942 article in *The Studio*. *Courtesy of the George Sakier Foundation.*

2.111 Neo-Classic champagnes.

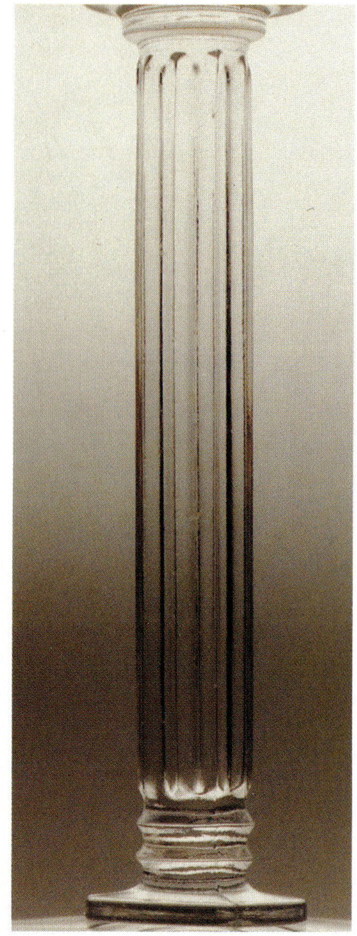

2.112 Detail of Neo-Classic stem.

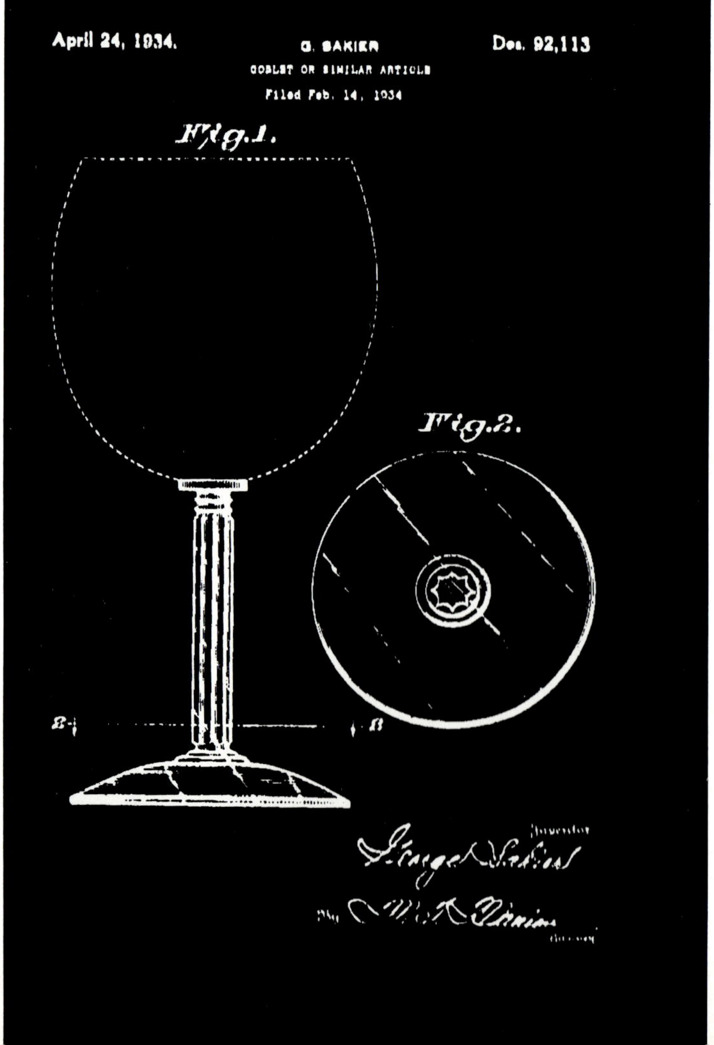

2.113 Patent drawing for Neo-Classic goblet, applied for Feb. 14, 1934, and issued April 24, 1934.

2.114 Left, 6012 Westchester champagne with ruby bowl, h. 5 in., 1935-42; right, Neo-Classic footed juice with ruby bowl, h. 4 1/2 in. Curiously, the patent for Westchester is in Edgar Bottome's name, even though it was a Sakier design and exhibited as such (see, for example, 2.137).

2.115 Detail of Westchester stem.

2.116 Detail of Neo-Classic stem.

2.117 4024 Victorian with 726 Meteor cutting (same as 702 Comet cutting), 10-oz. goblet, h. 5 1/2 in., 4-oz. cocktail, and roly poly. Although this was a Sakier design pictured in the Sept. 1933 issue of *Arts and Decoration*, the patent was issued to Edgar Bottome on Aug. 15, 1933.

2.118 Victorian cocktails with Meteor/ Comet cutting.

2.119 Roly poly glasses with Meteor/ Comet cutting.

2.120 Victorian goblets with Meteor/Comet cutting.

2.121 Detail of Victorian stem.

2.122 Patent drawing for a goblet not known to have been produced, applied for Jan. 20, 1931, and issued Mar. 24, 1932.

2.123 Sceptre sherbets in crystal, h. 4 1/2 in., 1937-71.

2.124 Sceptre sherbet with 767 Beacon cutting.

2.125 6017 Sceptre footed juice, h. 4 3/4 in., footed water, h. 6 in., and sherbet, h. 4 1/2 in., with gold tint bowls and crystal stems, 1937-43. These were pictured in the 1942 *Studio Yearbook.*

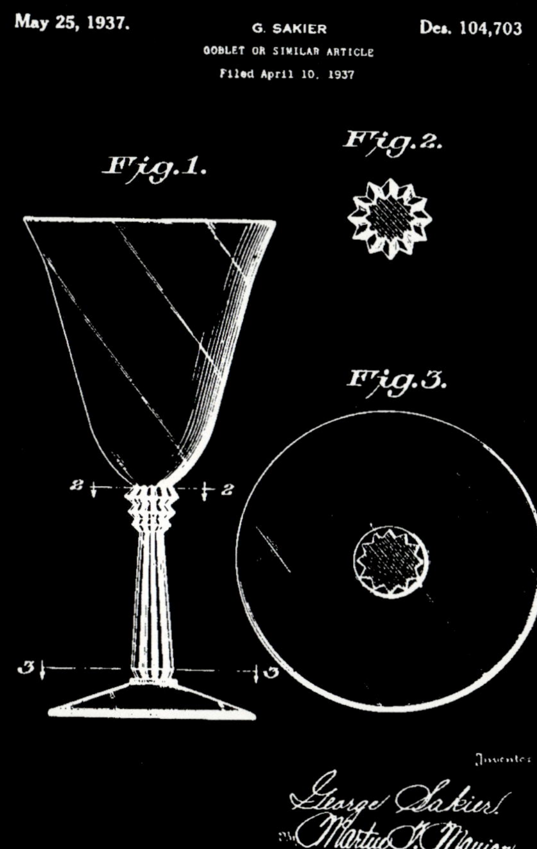

2.126 Patent drawing for Sceptre, applied for April 10, 1937, and issued May 25, 1937.

2.127 Detail of Sceptre stem.

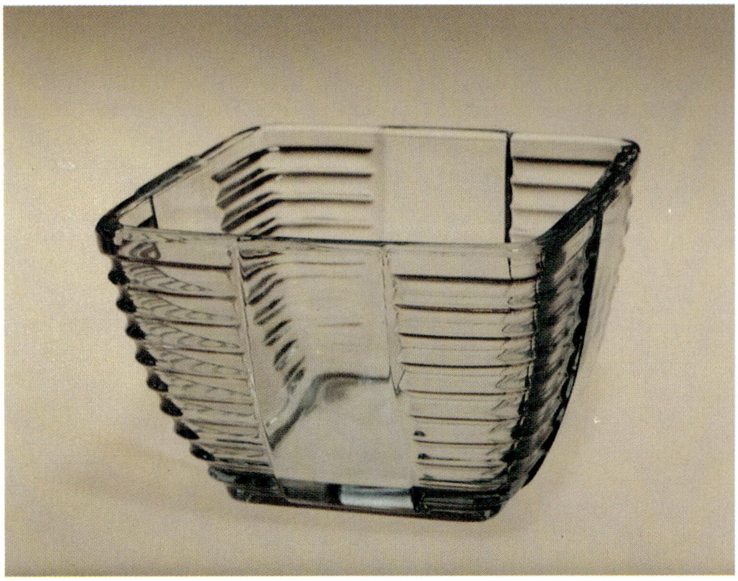

2.128 Number 2546 quadrangle bowl in blue, d. 4 1/2 in., attributed to Sakier (as are the matching candlesticks).

2.129 2550 Spool straight vase in gold tint (topaz), h. 5 3/4 in., pictured in the Jan. 1, 1937, Fostoria catalog and discontinued in 1944.

2.130 Spool round salad bowl in gold tint, d. 9 1/2 in.

Left: 2.131 6020 Melody low sherbet with 332 Mayflower plate etching, 1938-1954.

Below Left: 2.132 Pair of 2763 hurricane lamps with rope twist stems similar to stem design of the Melody pattern, designed in 1961 and still available in 1982. *Courtesy of the George Sakier Foundation.*

Below: 2.133 Single 2763 candlestick, identical to hurricane lamp but without the chimney, h. 9 1/4 in.

2.134 Pair of unidentified Fostoria candlesticks resembling wood turning. *Courtesy of the George Sakier Foundation.*

2.136 2594 Plume trindle and single candlesticks similar to handle design of Coronet, about 1940. *Courtesy of the George Sakier Foundation.*

2.135 2563 Viking bowl with wing handles, produced 1939-1943, total length 14 3/4 in. The 4 1/2-in. candlesticks of this pattern are pictured in the museum exhibit (2.137). *Identification courtesy of Gary Schneider.*

2.137 Shelves of Sakier designs for Fostoria exhibited at the Metropolitan Museum of Art and pictured in *U. S. Industrial Design 1949-1950. Courtesy of the George Sakier Foundation.*

2.138 2594 Plume trindle candlesticks, h. 7 3/4 in, w. 6 3/4 in.: front, plain; rear with 284 New Garland plate etching, 1930-34.

2.139 Detail of Plume.

2.140 2560 Coronet footed creamer and sugar with plume design for handles, 1938-60.

2.142 Detail of Coronet plume handle.

2.141 Detail of Coronet edge.

2.143 Coronet footed sugar with 333 Willowmere plate etching, and plain individual cream.

Top: 2.144 6027 Envoy stems, 1940-57. *Courtesy of the George Sakier Foundation.*

Left: 2.145 Detail of Envoy stem.

Above: 2.146 892 Nordic goblets, left example with 795 Papyrus cutting, 1939-43. *Courtesy of the George Sakier Foundation.*

2.147 Left, 6037 Silver Flutes footed juice, h. 4 in., 1949-71; center left, 6027 Envoy saucer champagne, h. 4 1/8 in., 1940-57; center right, 892 Nordic saucer champagne, h. 5 1/4 in.,1939-43; right, 6019 Rondel cocktail, h. 4 1/8 in., 1937-43.

2.148 Detail of Silver Flute stem.

2.149 Detail of Rondel stem.

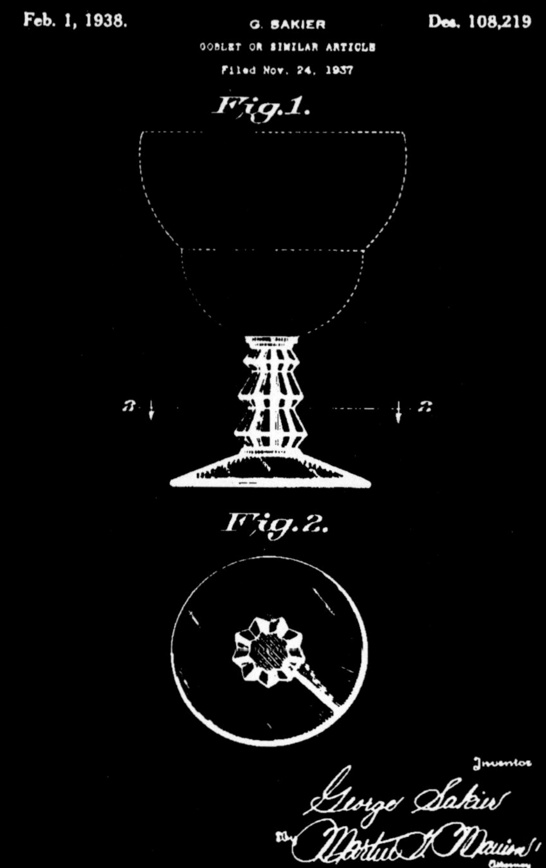

2.150 Patent drawing for Rondel, applied for Nov. 24, 1937, and issued Feb. 1, 1938.

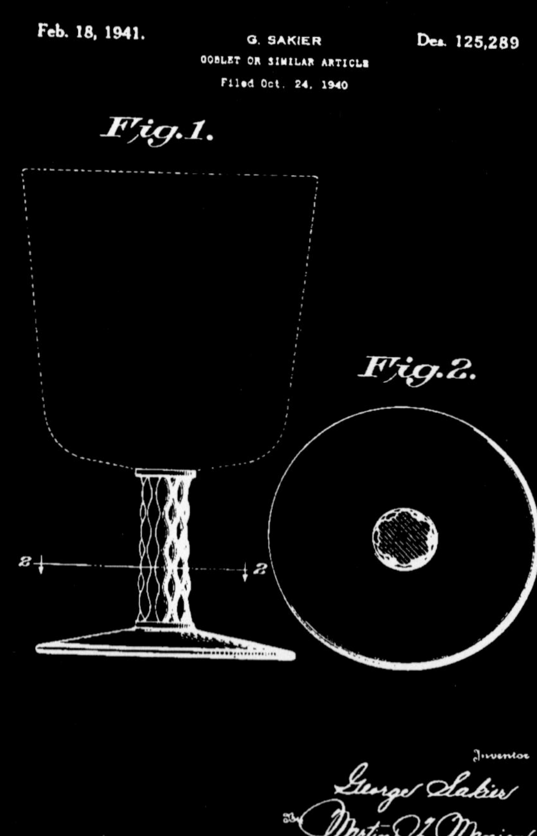

2.151 Patent drawing for Envoy, filed Oct. 24, 1940, and issued Feb. 18, 1941.

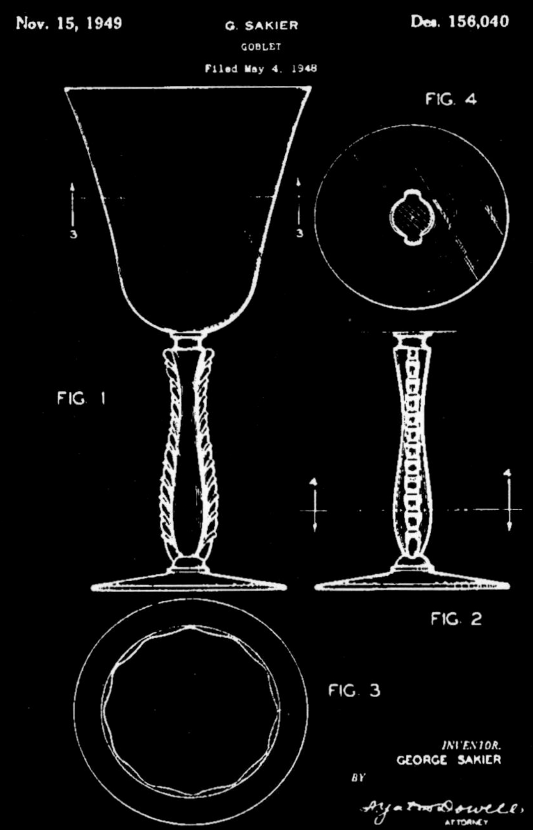

2.152 Patent drawing for Silver Flutes goblet, filed May 4, 1948, and issued Nov. 15, 1949.

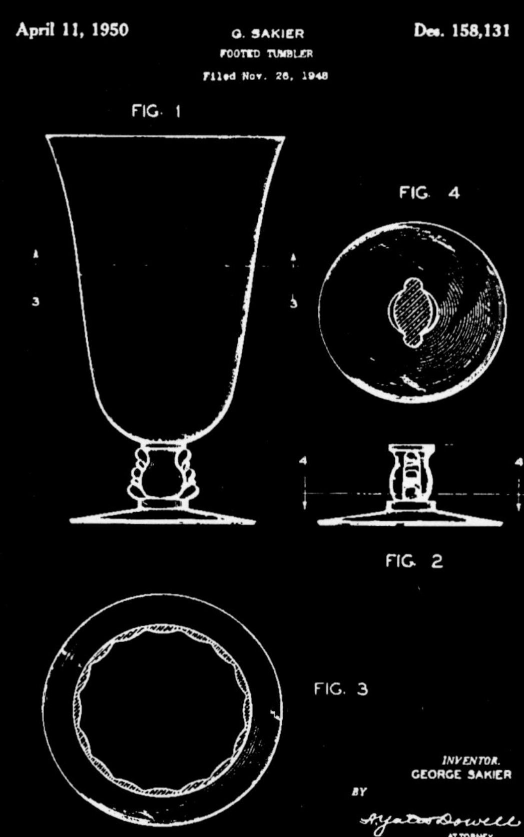

2.153 Patent drawing for Silver Flutes footed tumbler, applied for Nov. 26, 1948, and issued April 11, 1950. According to "References" of the patent text, the design was already illustrated in a Fostoria Glass Co. catalog in 1936 (p. 63 bottom row).

2.154 2412 Colony 7-in. plates, 1938-79.

Above Right: 2.155 Colony sherbets and footed bud vase.

2.156 Number 2538 place card holders, considered part of the Colony pattern.

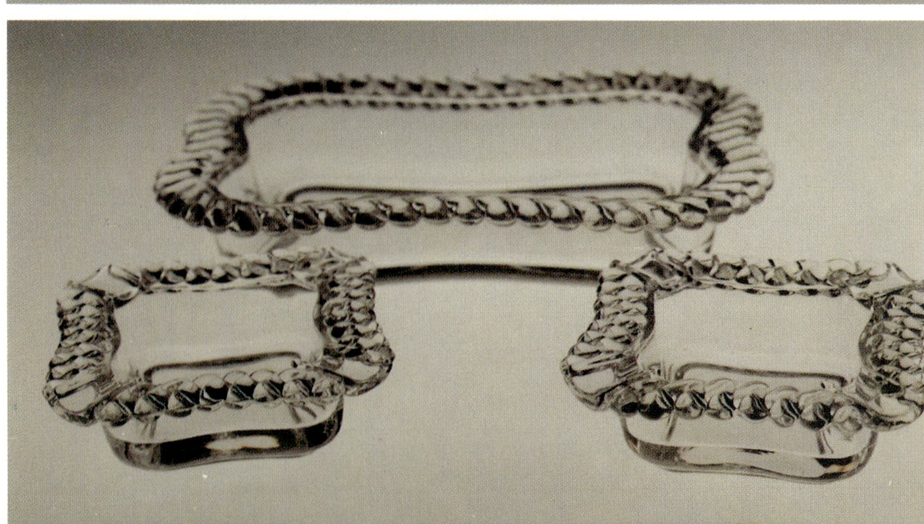

2.157 Colony individual ashtrays, l. 2 7/8 in., with pickle dish.

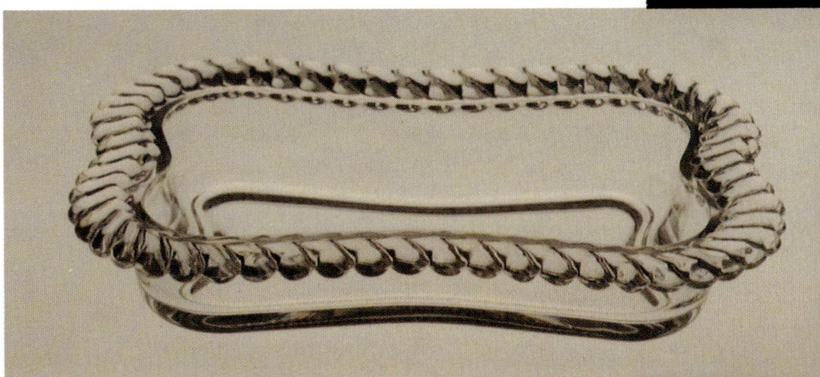

2.158 Colony rectangular pickle or olive dish, l. 6 1/4 in.

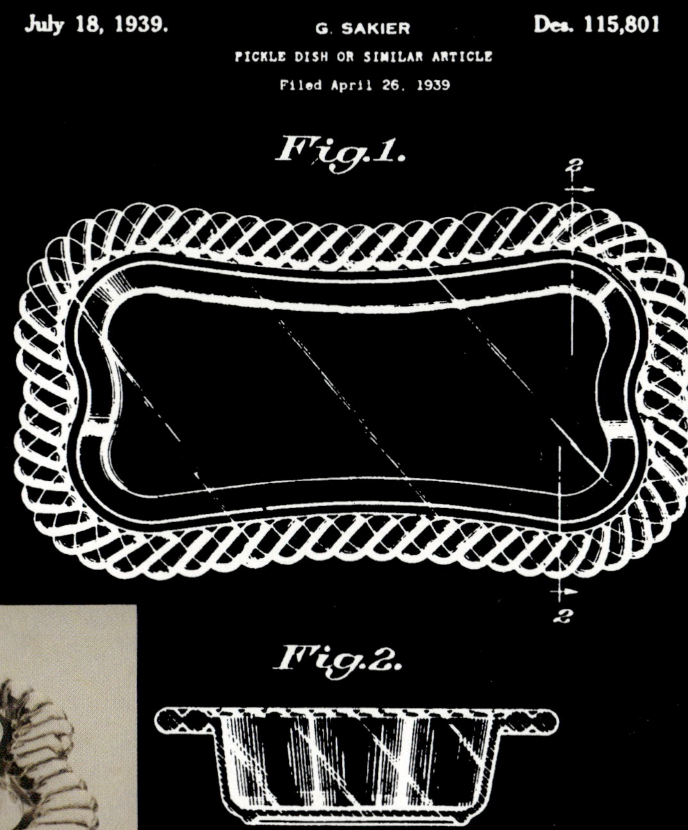

2.160 Patent drawing for pickle dish, filed April 26, 1939, and issued July 18, 1939.

2.159 Detail of pickle dish edge.

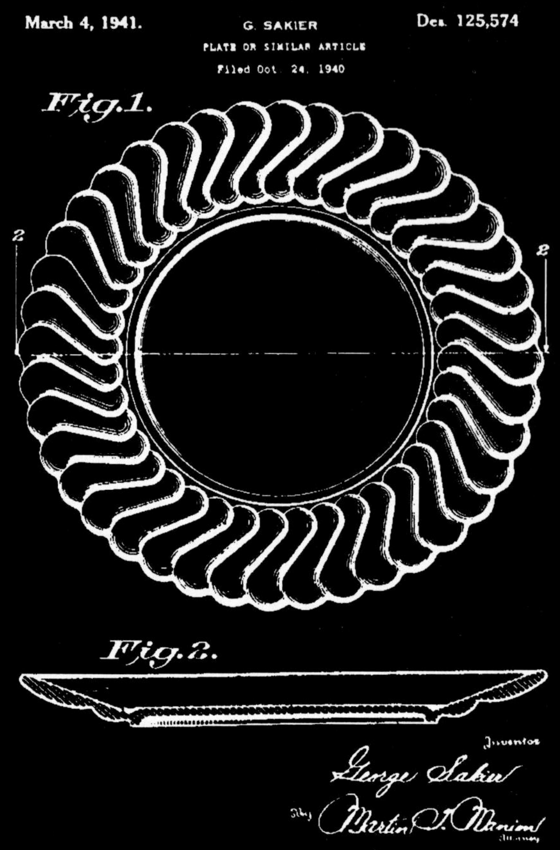

2.161 Patent drawing for plate, filed Oct. 24, 1940, and issued Mar. 4, 1941.

2.162 Patent drawing for goblet, filed Oct. 24, 1940, and issued Feb. 18, 1941.

2.163 Colony duo candlesticks, h. 6 1/8 in., w. 8 1/2 in.

2.164 Detail of candlestick.

2.165 2592 Myriad cigarette box with cover, l. 6 1/2 in., 1941-45, pictured in the Metropolitan Museum of Art exhibit that featured Sakier's glass.

2.166 Detail of Myriad.

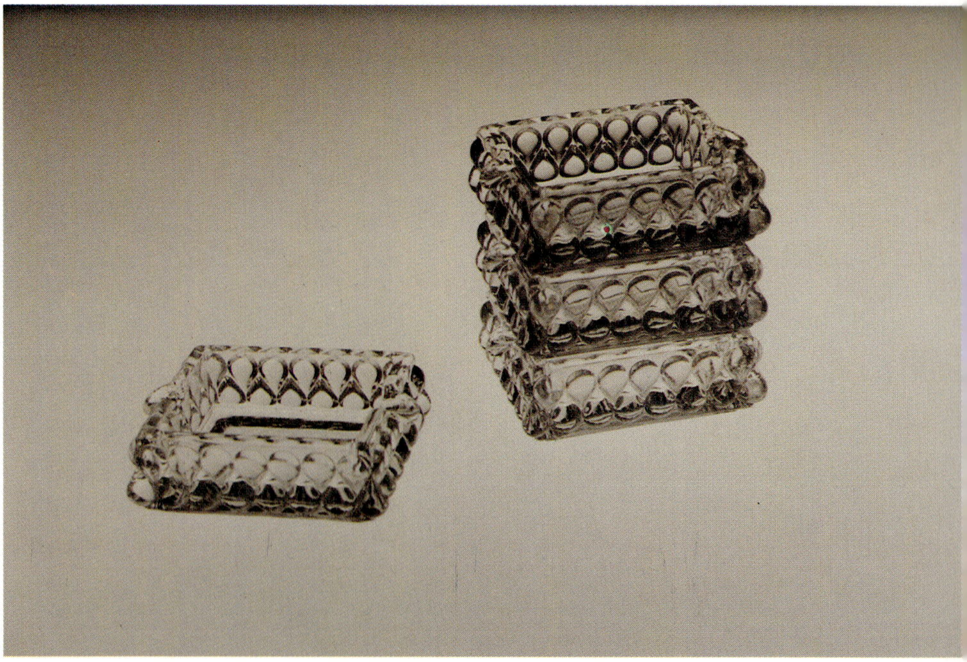

2.167 Myriad individual ashtrays, l. 3 in.

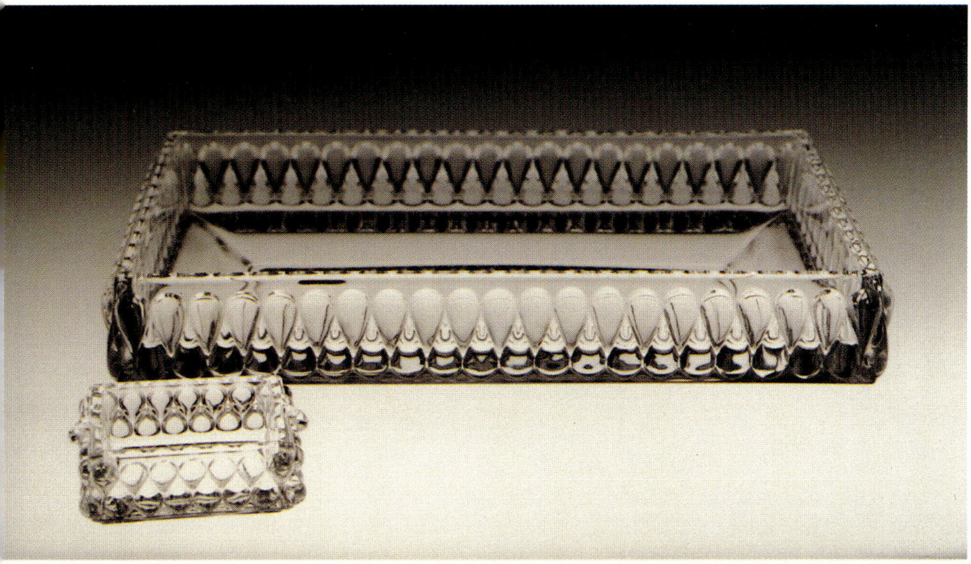

2.168 Myriad lily pond, l. 10 1/2 in., with individual ashtray.

2.169 Myriad double block candleholders, w. 6 5/8 in.

2.170 Myriad 4-in. ashtray in ebony with gold edge.

2.171 6030 Astrid stemware, 1942-74 and pictured in an article "Contemporary American Glass." *Courtesy of the George Sakier Foundation.*

2.172 Astrid claret-wines with 815 Holly cutting, 1942-74.

2.173 6033 Mademoiselle low sherbet with 821 Spinet cutting, 1950-60.

2.174 Detail of Mademoiselle stem.

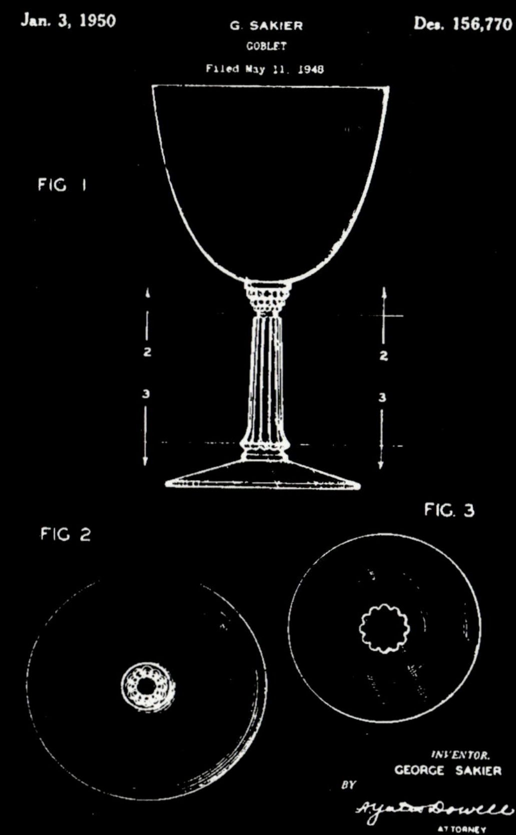

2.175 Patent drawing for Mademoiselle goblet, filed May 11, 1948, and issued Jan. 3, 1950.

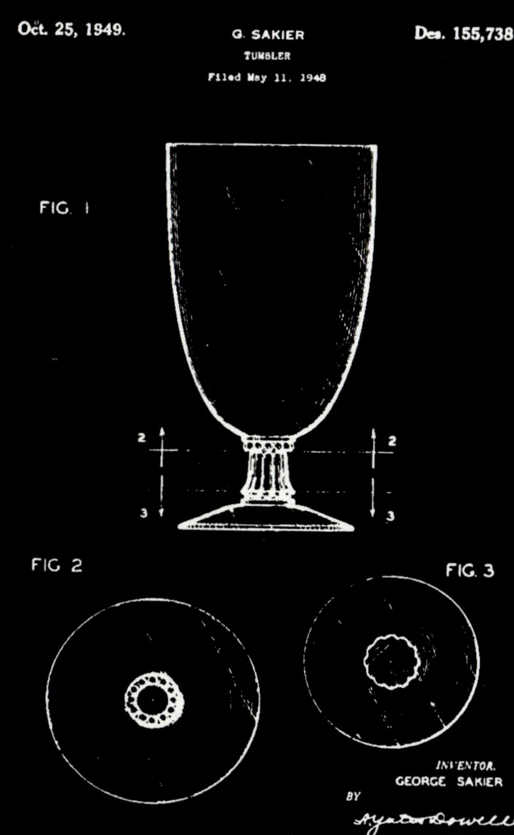

2.176 Patent drawing for Mademoiselle footed tumbler, filed May 11, 1948, and issued Oct. 25, 1949.

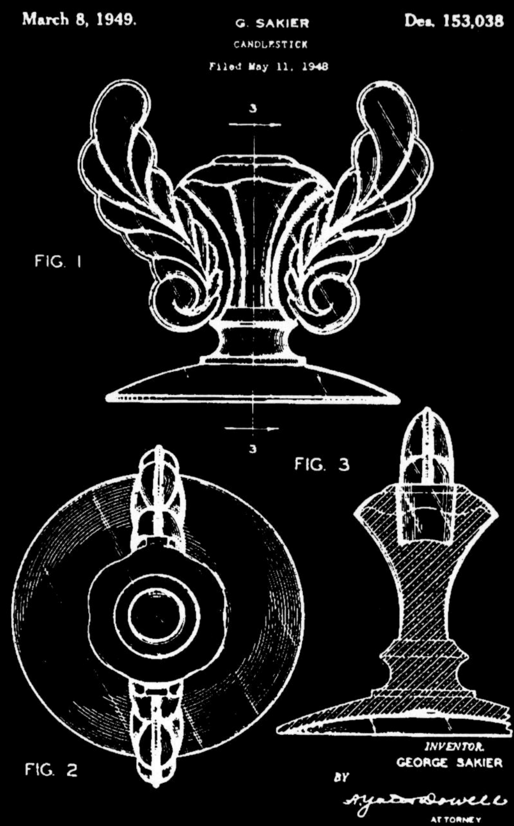

2.177 Patent drawing for another style of Plume candlestick, filed May 11, 1948, and issued Mar. 8, 1949.

2.178 Patent drawing for Plume handled bowl, filed May 11, 1948, and issued April 4, 1950.

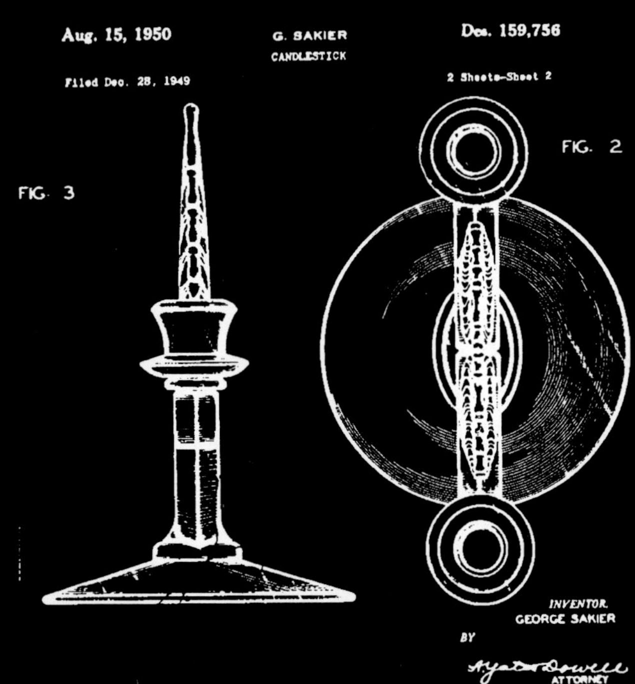

2.179 & 2.180 Patent drawing for Plume duo candlesticks, two views, filed Dec. 28, 1949, and issued Aug. 15, 1950.

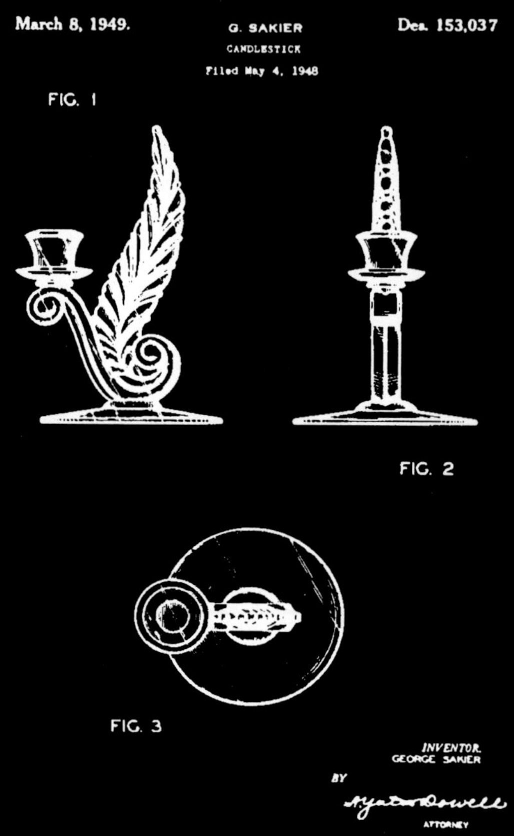

2.181 Patent drawing for Plume single candlestick, filed May 4, 1948, and issued Mar. 8, 1949.

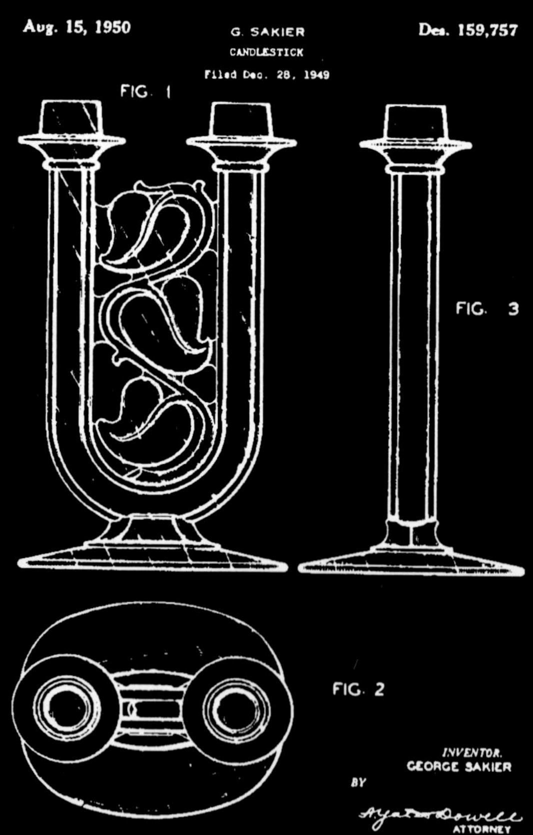

2.182 Patent drawing for 3639 Ivy duo candlestick, filed Dec. 28, 1949, and issued Aug. 15, 1950.

2.183 2746/118 ashtrays with tapered columnar bases: left, cracked ice finish in green; right, red test piece etched on the inside of the bowl in script, "color ok for this item w-ruby." This is one of the many smoking accessories Sakier designed in the 1950s. *Courtesy of the Huntington Museum of Art.*

2.184 2746 ruby ashtray from regular production with slight amberina effect at the base, d. 7 3/8 in., h. 3 1/2 in.

2.185 Detail of base.

Above: 2.186 5650 Horizon water tumbler with cinnamon bowl and crystal foot, h. 6 in.

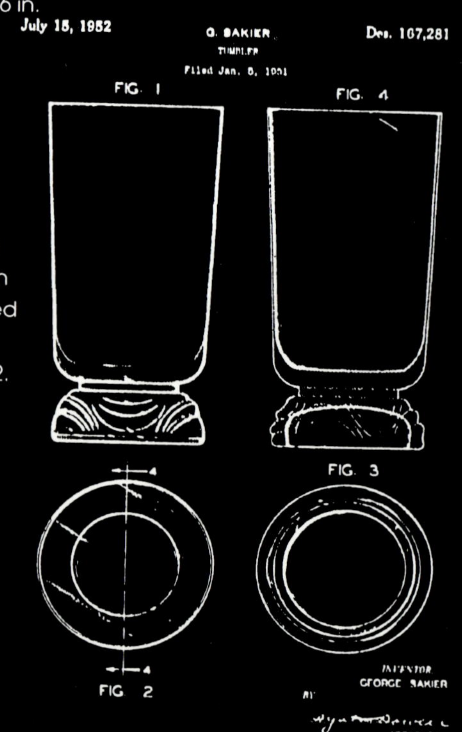

Right: 2.187 Patent drawing for Horizon footed tumbler, filed Jan. 5, 1951, and issued July 15, 1952.

Left: 2.188 Horizon sherbet/old fashioned and juice/cocktail in spruce, with cinnamon water/scotch and soda.

2.189 Horizon low tumblers, h. 5 1/4 in., with fruit bowls, d. 4 1/2 in., both in cinnamon with crystal bases.

2.190 Horizon sherbet/old fashioned with spruce bowl and crystal foot, h. 3 3/8 in., with early Fostoria paper label.

2.191 Detail of Horizon foot.

Above: 2.192 2650 Horizon cups and saucers in cinnamon, cup h. 2 3/8 in. Dinnerware is heavy pressed and is a different number from the blown tumblers.

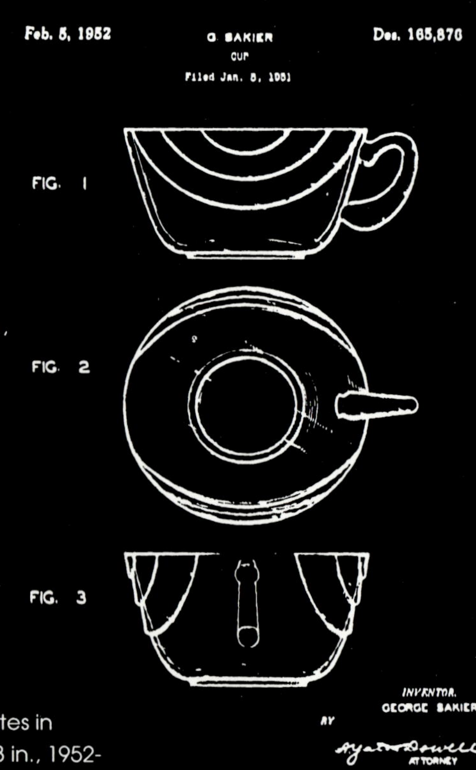

Right: 2.193 Patent drawing for Horizon cup, filed Jan. 5, 1951, and issued Feb. 5, 1952.

Left: 2.194 Horizon plates in spruce green, d. 7 3/8 in., 1952-55.

2.195 Horizon 3-part relish in green, l. 12 1/2 in.

2.196 Horizon 3-part relish in cinnamon.

2.197 Horizon salad bowl in cinnamon, d. 10 1/2 in.

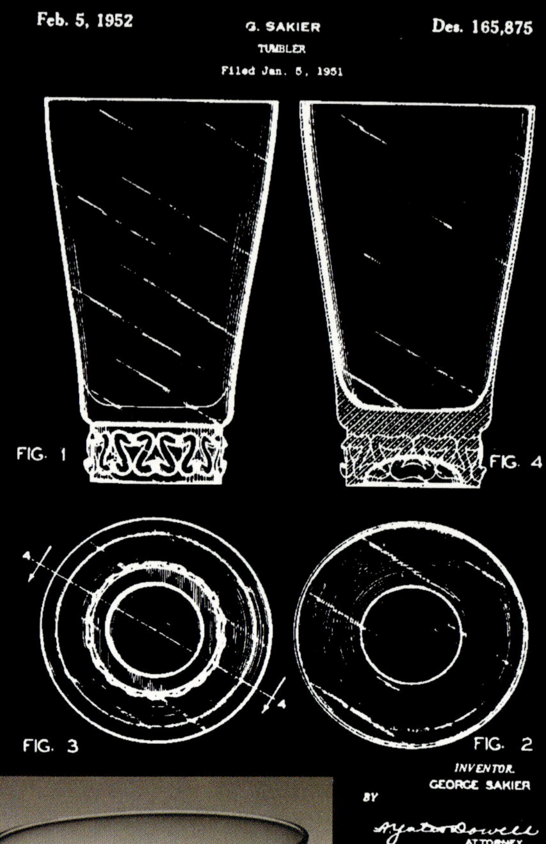

2.198 Patent drawing for Tiara, filed Jan. 5, 1951, and issued Feb. 5, 1952.

2.199 6044 Tiara blown tumblers: footed juice with cinnamon bowl and crystal base, h. 3 1/8 in.; ice tea with spruce bowl and crystal base, h. 5 7/8 in., 1950s.

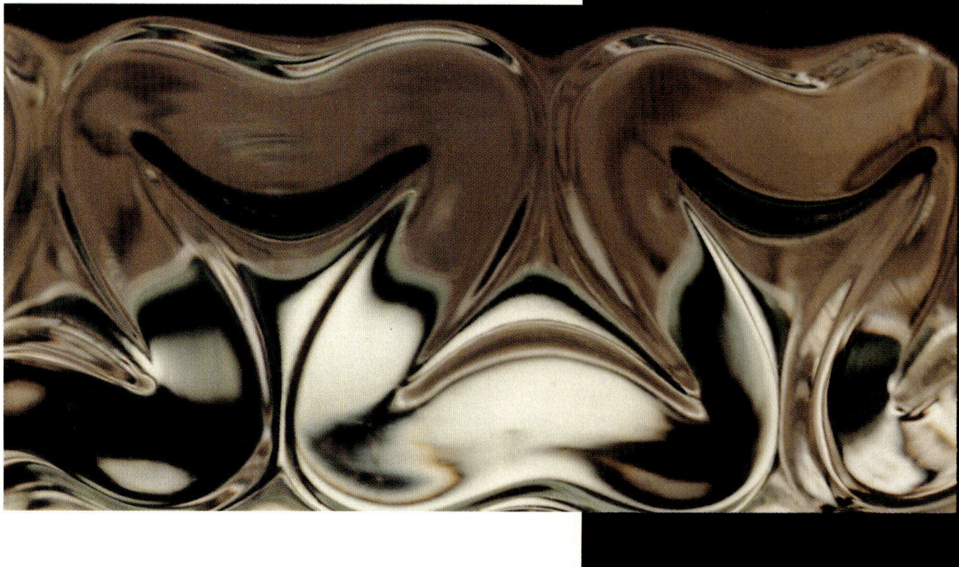

2.200 Detail of Tiara base.

2.201 6064 Patrician crystal blown lead glass sherbet, h. 4 7/8 in., 1956-71; example pictured in the Corning Museum of Glass exhibit catalog *Glass 1959*.

2.202 Variation of Patrician, this 6064 1/2 Elegance has a narrow rib optic: champagne h. 5 3/4 in., 1956-71.

2.203 Heavy pressed crystal 2718 Fairmont: left, goblet, h. 5 7/8 in.; right, footed ice tea, h. 6 1/2 in., 1958-65.

2.204 Detail of Fairmont.

Above Left: 2.205 Crystal goblet in 2719 Jamestown pattern, introduced in 1958 and produced until 1985.

Left: 2.206 Jamestown crystal jelly with cover, h. 6 in.

Above Right: 2.207 Jamestown sherbet in ruby.

2.208 2719 Jamestown water tumbler, footed juice, and goblet in amber.

2.209 Jamestown: left, amber juice, h. 4 3/4 in.; center, blue ice tea, h. 6 1/8 in.; right, crystal goblet, h. 5 3/4 in.

2.210 Crowns, another of Sakier's surprisingly traditional forms, designed in the late 1950s: 2749 Windsor, 2750 Hapsburg, and 2751 Navarre. Top, footed chalice and cover: gold Hapsburg, ruby Windsor, crystal Hapsburg, gold Windsor, and ruby Hapsburg; center, covered candy: royal blue Windsor, red Hapsburg, crystal Hapsburg, gold Windsor, and royal blue Hapsburg; bottom, Navarre 9-in. bowls in crystal and gold and footed bowl in crystal. *Courtesy of the George Sakier Foundation.*

2.211 The Coin pattern was introduced in 1958 (some items and colors came later) and produced at least until 1982. According to Fostoria author Ann Kerr, Sakier was responsible for designing the shapes;[9] some were adapted from earlier patterns and others were newly developed. There is a strong resemblance between the fussy traditional shapes of the Crowns he designed and several of the Coin items. Left, covered candy jar, h. 6 3/4 in.; center, creamer, h. 3 1/2 in.; right, covered sugar, h. 5 3/8 in., all in green, 1963-64. *Collection of Glenn and Betty Close.*

2.212 Blue Coin: left, low candy box with cover, h. 4 1/8 in., d. 6 3/8 in.; center, 8-in. bud vase; right, handled nappy, d. 5 3/8 in., all in blue, 1961-66. *Collection of Glenn and Betty Close.*

2.213 Amber coin: left, covered sugar, h. 5 3/8 in.; center, wedding bowl and cover, h. 8 3/16 in.; right, creamer, h. 3 1/2 in., 1963-82. *Collection of Glenn and Betty Close.*

2.214 Tall footed urn and cover in ruby, h. 12 3/4 in, 1967-81. *Collection of Glenn and Betty Close.*

2.215 Footed compote in olive green, d. 8 1/2 in., 1965-81. *Collection of Glenn and Betty Close.*

Top: 2.216 Pair of 2601 Lyre candleholders, very likely a Sakier design, h. 8 in., also made as bookends.

Above: 2.217 2601 Lyre centerpiece bowl, l. 13 1/4 in.

Right: 2.218 6113 Versailles blown crystal stemware, 1969-72: left, with 683 gold decoration on stem; right, 684 Moon Mist decoration on stem. *Courtesy of the George Sakier Foundation.*

2.219 Heavy pressed 2832 Sorrento, in colors green, blue, plum, brown, and pink, 1971-74. *Courtesy of the George Sakier Foundation.*

2.220 Detail of Sorrento stem.

2.221 Detail of Sorrento bowl.

2.222 Sorrento goblets in blue and plum, with pink sherbet.

2.223 Sorrento sherbets in plum, pink, and blue.

2.225 Sorrento green sherbets, h. 3 5/8 in.

2.224 Sorrento green: left, tumbler, h. 5 5/8 in.; center left, goblet, h. 6 in.; right front, wine, h. 4 7/8 in., right, footed ice tea, h. 6 3/4 in., all with paper labels.

2.226 Sorrento 8-in. plate in brown, actual d. 8 5/8 in., with paper label FOSTORIA SORRENTO.

2.227 Sorrento brown sherbets, h. 3 5/8 in.

Chapter Three: Industrial Design

Americans are fascinated by superlatives: biggest, smallest, fastest, best, earliest (first). Norman Bel Geddes is credited with opening the first industrial design office in 1927; Joseph Sinel claimed to be the first established industrial designer in the United States; in 1934 *Fortune* magazine listed George Sakier as having been in the field since 1923.[1] Then consider Michael Thonet, nineteenth-century inventor of the process for making bentwood furniture and the machines for mass-producing it. Earlier still, Richard Arkwright's English patent for a spinning machine was dated 1769. Perhaps we should go further back in time to Renaissance genius Leonardo da Vinci, artist, engineer, architect, and research scientist who drew plans for a flying machine. These individuals also designed for industry even if, as in the case of da Vinci, the industry would not exist for centuries.

Yet Sakier and a handful of other designers have been credited with pioneering a new field that was developing in the United States during the Depression years of the 1930s. This new field was dependent upon materials and technologies that had not previously existed. It drew for its aesthetic philosophy from an equally new phenomenon, abstract art. Though it may not have been fashionable to admit at the time, they were also influenced by the opulent, elitist, and craft-driven French Art Moderne, which had been transplanted onto American soil via fashion and merchandising. Designers from a variety of primarily two-dimensional design backgrounds were called upon to add style to both new and existing items. As industrial design historians Sheldon and Martha Cheney wrote: "The most obvious style mark, the streamline, came from the one totally ancestorless invention, the airplane. Most rapid progress had occurred in connection with those commodities that are either substantially new things in the world or also so essentially utilitarian that they had escaped artistic treatment before."[2]

In the past, machines had been designed by engineers or proto-engineers without art training and then decorated, if at all, by artists. Neither the engineers nor the artists necessarily understood each other, and it was the artists or machine decorators who were the most severely criticized. One explanation for the problem, according to Cheney, was in the choice of decoration. The record of art in — or rather on — the machine and its products was until the 1920s almost exclusively one of inappropriate borrowing. On both sides of the Atlantic the impulse to decorate persisted. "All cultural periods of the past had long been raided, and their treasures reduced to patterns, numbered ready to be laid on to the machine and its products"[3]. Forms were obscured rather than enhanced by these embellishments. There was an aesthetic time warp: neither the machine-made objects nor the machines of the Industrial Revolution looked very revolutionary, because familiar historic revivalist motifs of handicraft were arbitrarily applied to both.

From a vantage point of having seen both modern twentieth-century industrial design (though not yet defined here) and a nineteenth-century version of industrial design, the latter can still be appreciated and enjoyed for different reasons, not excluding an acquired taste for camp. Industrial design as it emerged in the late 1920s was not machine decoration, but machine art. Just as past styles reflected their respective cultures, so would the new styles reflect modern culture. These new styles were also affected by twentieth-century crafting techniques, namely, mass production. This mass production required a different set of aesthetic values plus a means to market them to the consumer. At least two significant influences can be credited to two-dimensional art: abstraction in painting, something only a specialized minority had access to, and graphic design, which had already absorbed and synthesized elements of both abstract art and the often-criticized but freely copied French Art Moderne.

This modern art was not only aesthetically sensible for mass-produced design, it made perfect sense functionally and economically. Essentially geometric forms were lifted from a two-dimensional context to fill three-dimensional space. Not just any art — Modern art — was injected into, rather than applied onto, industrial design; the design came from the inside out. As one contemporary writer put it: "Two apparently irreconcilable and antithetical extremes of human ingenuity meet and are reconciled in this new figure: heavy, commercial, systematized technics and theoretical, abstract, pure art."[4] So then, we have a definition: mass production + abstract art = industrial design. Modernist design becomes the machine aesthetic, and the practitioners of the new field of industrial design who spoke the language of Modern art became pioneer Modernists in a new medium.

Since industrial design was not just transformed, but new in the 1930s, its pioneering practitioners came from somewhere else. Most came with education and/or experience in two-dimensional arts: theater set design, painting, illustration, advertising, and packaging design. Modern styles of the 1920s, particularly those being imported from Europe, touched those areas first. When artists and designers moved from two-dimensional stylization and abstraction into three-dimensional formats they carried this modernism to industry. They also brought along the know-how to market it. Since they already knew how to make the dimensional move, some continued to design theater sets or product packages as well. After all, once the principles of design are understood, travel between fields should not pose a problem.

In order to understand Sakier's part in this complex and significant cultural event, it will be helpful to know some of his peers, many of whom also worked in New York.

Egmont Arens (1888-1966) was a typesetter and then a magazine editor in Albuquerque, New Mexico in 1916; after moving to New York, he headed the industrial styling division of Calkins-Holden Advertising from 1929 to 1933. Arens became a leading packaging designer of coffee bags for the A & P food chain and items for Bristol-Myers, Aluminum Company of America (Alcoa), Seeman Bros., and Louis L. Libby. Product designs included electrical switches for Federal Electric Products, lamps, coffee mills, meat slicers, dishwashers, scales, mixers for Kitchen Aid, and other electric appliances.

Donald Deskey (1894-1989) was one of the first to integrate modern art into advertising design and manufactured products and also one of the first to introduce tubular steel furniture in the United States. Originally from Minnesota, he studied at Mark Hopkins Institute (California School of Fine Arts), the University of California at Berkeley, and in Paris. After serving in the military, he moved to New York in 1921 to work in advertising, but since his work was considered too modern, he opened his own agency. After traveling to Paris twice, he worked in the Art Moderne style for stage sets, furniture, and screens. Best known for the interior of Radio City Music Hall, he developed a striated fir plywood called Weldtex, did the first modern interior for an American ocean liner, the S. S. Argenta, and designed items such as pianos, billiard tables, clocks, office equipment, silverware, oil burners, radios, glassware, and slot machines, as well as package designs for Procter & Gamble.

Donald Dohner (1893-?) taught design at Carnegie Mellon University where he is credited with establishing the first American educational program in industrial design. He also began a similar program at Pratt Institute in 1935, was a free lance designer and worked for Westinghouse.

Henry Dreyfuss (1904-1972) was born in New York, learned to design theater sets under Bel Geddes, and opened his own industrial design firm in New York in 1929. He designed telephones for Bell Telephone Laboratories, vacuums for Hoover, clocks for Western Clock, oil drilling rigs for National Supply Co., farm machinery for Deere and Co., china lavatories for Crane Co., aircraft interiors for Lockheed and Boeing, and the spill-proof lunch trays to use during flight. He worked for Sears Roebuck, designed the streamlined Hudson train locomotive, construction equipment, washing machines, refrigerators, thermos bottles, a hook for amputees, typewriters, pens, pencils, and flyswatters. It was said that for years he liked to design for a Broadway show each season because his clients liked to see his name in theater programs. Dreyfuss also pioneered in the field of ergonomics.

Norman Bel Geddes (1893-1958) studied briefly at the Art Institute of Chicago, then worked in advertising, theatrical arts, painting, illustrating, exhibit design, set design, architecture and industrial design. He was called the P. T. Barnum of industrial design because of his showmanship. Among his many designs were scales for Toledo Scale, radio cabinets for Philco, a Graham Page automobile, and the Futurama exhibit for General Motors at the 1939 New York World's Fair.

Lurelle Guild (1898-?) graduated from Syracuse University in fine arts and went into acting, painting, advertising art, and illustration. His experience in theater and advertising led to industrial design, where he became so prolific that he held patents for more products than any other designer. His designs included refrigerators for Norge, vacuum cleaners for Electrolux, and items for Wear-Ever Aluminum.

Raymond Loewy (1893-1986) was born in Paris, where he studied engineering and enjoyed sketching locomotives and airplanes. He served in the French Army Corps of Engineers during World War I and became a highly decorated captain. When he left France in 1919 he memorized the New York City street map on the trip across the Atlantic. His first jobs in the United States were for major New York department stores dressing windows. He did fashion drawings for *Vogue*, *Vanity Fair*, and *Harper's Bazaar* magazines, designed costumes for Ziegfeld, and went into product design in the late 1920s and opened his own office in 1929. Designs included the Coldspot refrigerator for Sears Roebuck, buses for Greyhound, Studebaker and Huppmobile automobiles, airplane interiors for Curtiss-Wright, Douglas, and Boeing, speedboats, the S-1 locomotive for the Pennsylvania Railroad, the bottle for Coca-Cola, the package for Lucky Strike, corporate logos for British Petroleum, Shell, and Exxon, Air Force One for President Kennedy, and Skylab interiors for NASA.

Gilbert Rohde (1894-1944) was born in New York where he learned cabinetmaking at his father's shop and was considered a pioneer industrial designer in 1927. He designed furniture for Herman Miller where he developed modular and sectional furniture. He also designed furniture for Kroehler, Valentine Seaver, Troy Sunshade, and Heywood-Wakefield, as well as clocks for Howard Miller, water coolers, boilers, pianos, stokers, gas ranges, and exhibits in the Chicago World's Fair, Texas Centennial, San Francisco Golden Gate Exhibition, and the New York World's Fair. He headed the industrial design program at the New York School of Architecture from 1939 to 1943.

Joseph Sinel (1889-1975) came to the United States from New Zealand via Australia and England in 1918, was trained in lithography and illustration, became a leading trademark and packaging designer, and wrote *A Book of American Trademarks and Devices* in 1923. He also claimed to be the first established industrial designer in the United States.

Walter Dorwin Teague (1883-1960) was born in Indiana. He attended evening classes at the Art Students League in New York 1903 to 1907, did freelance drawing and sign lettering, joined the Ben Hampton Advertising Agency in 1908, then joined the Calkins-Holden agency, and in 1911 started his own office. His advertising designs included the Metropolitan Museum of Art industrial art exhibit in 1922. After going to Paris, he returned in the mid 1920s and concentrated on product designs such as cameras (notably the Baby Brownie) for Eastman Kodak; he designed A.B. Dick showrooms, weather instruments for Taylor Instrument Co., dinnerware for Taylor, Smith & Taylor, passenger cars for the New Haven Railroad, and Texaco service stations. He was on the Board of Design for the New York World's Fair and designed exhibits for Consolidated Edison, Ford Motors, United States Steel, du Pont, National Cash Register, Eastman Kodak, and A. B. Dick. In 1944 Teague became the first president of the newly formed Society of Industrial Designers (SID). Later designs included pens for Scripto, cans for Schaefer Beer, and 707 interiors for Boeing.

Harold Van Doren (1895-1957) was born in Chicago, studied painting in Europe, and worked at the Louvre. He returned to the United States and became an assistant at the Minneapolis Institute of Art, and opened a design office in the late 1920s in partnership with John Gordon Rideout (d. 1951); clients included Toledo Scale, Swartzbaugh Mfg. Co., Air King Products, Maytag, Goodyear Tire, Philco, and DeVilbiss. He was known for using Art Deco and streamlining, and designed streamlined tricycles for American National. In 1940 he wrote *Industrial Design:*

A Practical Guide.

John Vassos (1898-1985) was born in Greece and trained in commercial art, drew political cartoons for his father's newspaper in Constantinople, left Turkey in 1915, fought in the war for Britain, and came to the United States in 1919. He studied art and illustration at the Art Students League and with John Singer Sargent in Boston and John Sloan in New York. He did illustrations for magazines such as *Harper's* and *The New Yorker.* His first industrial design was a cosmetic bottle in 1924, and then he worked for clients such as RCA and Coca-Cola. Vassos helped found the American Designers Institute (ADI).

Russel Wright (1904-1976) was born in Ohio and was a child prodigy painter. In 1920 he studied at the Cincinnati Academy of Art, and then at the Art Students League in New York, where he also began designing theater costumes and sets. A versatile designer, Wright became best known for interior furnishings and domestic items such as the first modern blond maple furniture for Conant Ball. He designed glassware for Imperial Glass Co., Old Morgantown Glass Guild, and Fostoria Glass Co. Some of his best known designs were for pottery, especially the enormously successful American Modern dinnerware for Steubenville Pottery Co. (1939-1959), plus Iroquois Casual for Iroquois China Co. and lines for other pottery companies — Padden City, Sterling China, Harker, Edwin M. Knowles, and Bauer Art Pottery. He also designed streamlined radios for Wurlitzer, metalware for Chase Brass and Copper, spun aluminum items, cocktail gadgets, pianos, chewing gum dispensers, linotype machines, packaging, and World's Fairs exhibits.

All of these men, including Sakier, had art backgrounds, whether by studying, teaching, or practicing. Consumers were far less vocal about engineering deficiencies than they were about the dreary appearance of useful items. They placed a high value on appearance and demanded more than applied design clichés. Although it would seem that if the goal was to design from the inside out, and a designer with engineering skills had an obvious advantage, Sakier was almost alone with his background in engineering as a road to industrial design.

Deskey, Teague, Wright, and Sakier went to Paris and returned with Modern art, including one with a French accent — Art Moderne. The famous, or infamous, L'Exposition des Arts Décoratifs et Industriels Modernes held in Paris in 1925 was the first real exposure most Americans had to modern design. It was no coincidence that shortly after the Paris Expo, in the late 1920s, both the modernist movement (introduced in 1913 at the Armory Show) and the field of industrial design came alive in New York.

In retrospect, it is ironic that an elitist style, accused of being shallow and seductive (not to mention occasionally a bit bizarre and kinky), that entered the United States via department stores and museums, would have so strong an influence on a budding profession professing to be born from engineering and pure abstract art. French Art Moderne decorative arts — furniture, screens, art glass, ceramics, metalware, jewelry — were excessively costly because their production methods and producers represented the antithesis of industrial design. The French took rare and exotic materials, used traditional handicraft methods, and made sumptuous objects. Many of the modernists, especially architects who were often from or influenced by the Bauhaus, had Socialist leanings, so any blatantly upperclass French fashion was rejected as much on philosophical as aesthetic grounds. The designs, nonetheless, if one really looked at them, were extraordinary.

Regardless of politics, the designs were modern. Neoclassical references or not, the highly stylized and bold motifs and shapes were very new and refreshing. They were also relatively easy to reduce to clichés and copy. It wasn't long before American manufacturers began to indiscriminately apply Art Moderne symbols to cheap mass-produced goods, not unlike the way they had once cluttered them with fruits and flowers. Though the 1851 Crystal Palace exhibition seemed like a long way off, an echo of its exhibit catalog could still be heard: "ornament is now as material an interest in a commercial community as the raw materials of manufacture itself."[5]

The new ornament indeed carried commercial interest. Eventually it was reduced to what Martin Greif calls "the strange cult of the three little lines, three parallel lines intended to suggest modernity." These and the aerodynamic streamline shape and line — a curved line with a sharp parabolic curve at one end — became "a way of marketing items which were never intended with speed in mind."[6]

There was also an upside to the new style or styles introduced through European decorative arts. Though the leaders and followers of Art Moderne were usually not industrial designers, they "helped to provide a design vocabulary expressive of the tempo of America's new machine age that could be applied by others to consumer products."[7] These "others" were the industrial designers who were able to translate the new design vocabulary from French to American. There was nothing inherently wrong with the three little parallel lines, the streamline, rounded corners, or classical references of Art Moderne (to the contrary, many would consider them to be very right), as long as their application to mass-produced goods was appropriate. Consumers, tired of dreary looking goods, would have their day. Streamlined form and the streamline symbol were right for trains, planes, ships, and automobiles. Though it may have been stretching the point to streamline an electric iron, consumers voted "yes" at the ultimate ballotbox, the marketplace. Sales of newly-styled items often increased twofold, even sixfold. Thanks to efficient design and mass-production techniques, industry could reduce costs at one end, while increasing sales at the other. If the industrial designers were even partly responsible for the huge profits, then they had earned their keep, and in the 1930s, top industrial designers were among the highest paid professionals in America.

Not copyists of either abstract painting or of modern decoration, the designers for industry were giving birth to a new art form. Its vocabulary included what was modern in the fine and decorative arts, as well as engineering, and even marketing. Since most came with training and expertise in art and advertising, their immediate successes were not random and of no surprise. These designers were multi-talented, plus they were in exactly the right place at exactly the right time. Greif went so far as to write, "Few generations have better understood themselves and their times than the designers of the '30s. They knew what they were creating, they knew why they were creating it, and they even had a premonition of what their place in history would be because they had created it." Yet, when asked to predict what housing would be like in the next century, Sakier rather insightfully answered, "It is impossible to predict the future in design unless one knows social changes."[8] Indeed, for the decade in question was to see the rise of totalitarianism and World War II.

3.1 "Futuristic Design" featured in the Feb. 1939 issue of *Vogue*. Caption reads "Wide conditioning belt to receive high frequency radiations will be feature of skirtless costumes of women of the future." *Copyright 1939 (renewed 1967) by the Condé Nast Publications Inc., photo, Anton Bruehl, courtesy Vogue.*

Industrial designers were frequently asked to make predictions. Their place on the proverbial cutting edge, their future oriented stance, prompted *Vogue* magazine to invite nine prominent industrial designers who were at the time designing exhibits and buildings at the 1939 New York World's Fair—Egmont Arens, Donald Deskey, Henry Dreyfuss, Raymond Loewy, Joseph Platt, Gilbert Rohde, George Sakier, Walter Dorwin Teague, and Russel Wright — to have some fun with predictions outside of their usual fields. Each was asked to design a futuristic costume for women for the year 2000. These predictions were then executed by leading New York fashion houses, and each one was featured as a color page of the February 1939 issue of *Vogue.*

Fashion was no stranger to Sakier, who had served as art director of French *Vogue* in the mid 1920s (he resigned because of difficulty with the French language), followed by a similar position at *Modes and Manners* and then *Harper's Bazar* in the late 1920s (when Bazar was spelled with one 'a'). In a letter written in 1930, *Bazaar* editor Charles Hanson Towne called Sakier's work "among the best that we have ever had." The title for Sakier's design in the 1939 *Vogue* read "No Mechanistic Clothes for Future Women Predicts George Sakier." He predicted that in the distant future, women's clothing would be "simple and free from fantasy...on all her costumes, a wide belt is worn — a hypothetical receptor for high-frequency radiations, emanating from a central source. These are to adapt the body to temperature and altitude changes, by regulating circulation and respiration."[9] Sakier's interest in female physiology was not limited to futuristic fashion fantasies; his fondness for the ladies was well known.

In an undated article about plumbing design, Sakier wrote, "At dinner, when my partner feels it is about time to ask what I do, I generally, albeit I have more romantic wares to offer, answer that I design bathtubs. The response is electric, earnest, and most gratifying. I am now sure of her complete attention for at least three courses. My hostess beams and forgives me for not playing bridge. I become a social asset."[10] Even the trivial became newsworthy if it concerned industrial designers, and Sakier's playfulness seems to have been picked up by another writer. In a 1935 article in *Arts and Decoration* the author wrote: "It is no age however in which to take plumbing fixtures casually. They may have been designed by the man whose painting hangs on your picture gallery wall...George Sakier had made dinner table conversation of plumbing. He has made both more interesting."[11]

Before making a niche by designing modern (typically covered by the umbrella term Art Deco since the late 1960s when it was coined) bath fixtures that he named Neo-Classic, Sakier designed (gasp) ornate period bathrooms with lavish gold trimming on otherwise excellent plumbing. These luxurious ensembles, with oversized tubs with wide deep seats at one end and gold taps at another, could cost as much as $7,000.[12] When the luxury market all but disappeared in 1929, Sakier switched to designing only minimum-sized maximum efficiency "machines for cleanliness" not unlike Le Corbusier's "machines for living." In the bathroom, Sakier had made the jump from decorative art to industrial design.

An economic climate that gives rise to tremendous competition for a market share is one where the total market is small; this small market may not be due to any lack of desire to purchase products, but on a lack of money. An economic depression is such a climate, and the Great Depression of the 1930s was when industrial design came into being, because

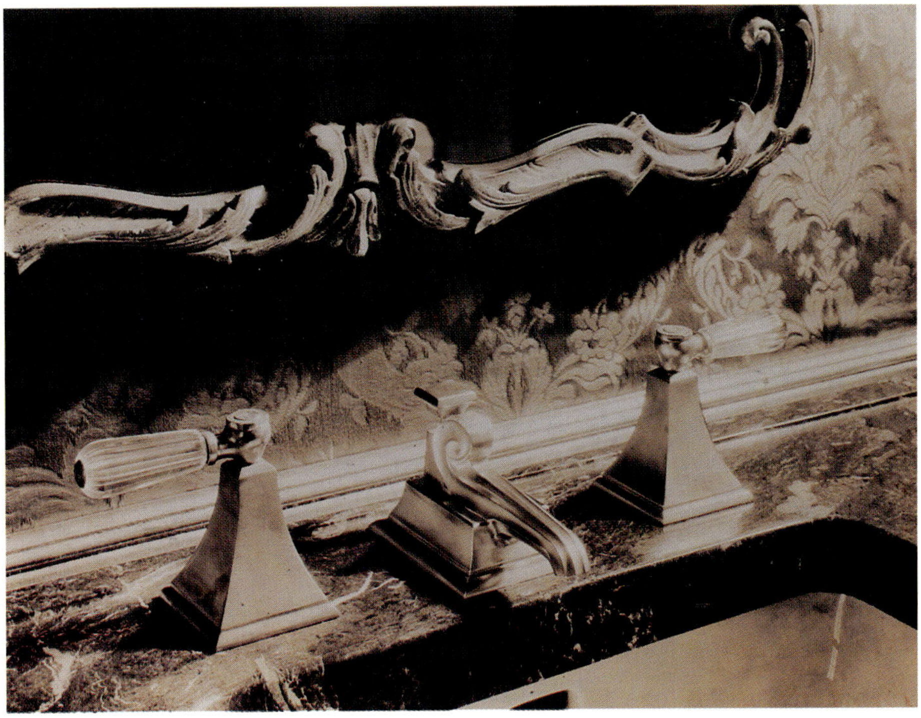

3.2 Faucet mounted on black marble sink top. *Courtesy of the George Sakier Foundation.*

consumers required not just low cost and practical use from their goods, they also wanted appearance. Beyond superficial ornament, they wanted good-looking design integral to the item's function that also contributed to ease of manufacture and resultant low cost. It was a tall order. Industrial design may have been art, but first, having been born in the Depression, it was business. Designers coming directly from advertising brought their marketing know-how, and others learned on the job. In 1940 Harold Van Doren defined the industrial designer's job: "to interpret the function of useful things in terms of appeal to the eye; to endow them with beauty of form and color; above all to create in the consumer the desire to possess. To accomplish these things one needs not only talent but technique." This "desire to possess" was the bottom line; the industrial designer's primary goal was to instill this desire. Van Doren's definition of industrial design is similar but worth mentioning: "Industrial design is concerned with three-dimensional products or machines made only by modern production methods as distinguished from traditional handcraft methods. Its purpose is to enhance their desirability in the eyes of the purchaser through increased convenience and better adaptability of form to function through a shrewd knowledge of consumer psychology and through the aesthetic appeal of form, color, and texture."[13] Whatever noble causes industrial designers might also have had, their purpose was to sell the product by making it look irresistible.

The appearance factor became eminently clear in 1927 when the man who said "They can have it in any color so long as its black" gave in to the reality of the appearance factor. After buying fifteen million Tin Lizzies, the public tired of black. In order to compete with General Motors and other companies, Henry Ford had to revamp his facilities at great expense. The emerging concept of planned obsolescence depended on the consumer's desire for newness. At the same time, the system of mass-production and interchangeable parts made it even more profitable.

Sakier was aware that if parts became obsolete at a rapid rate, the value of the whole investment would be impaired. He was criticized for having a "locked door" policy, whereby new designs sat behind the door waiting to be introduced. Since, for example, a bathtub was intended to last, the lag between new tub designs was typically three to ten years. On the other hand, molded glassware (ie., his Fostoria designs) had a lag of only about six months.[14] New glass designs could be continually introduced

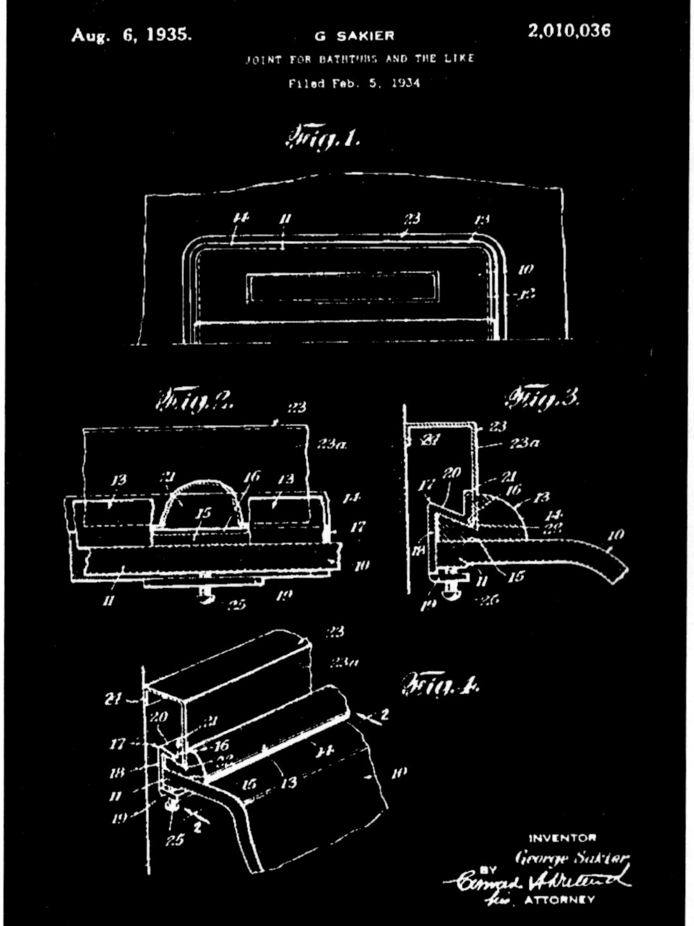

3.3 Patent drawing of bathtub joint: provides a simple, efficient, and inexpensive means for forming water-tight joints between the edges or rims of bathtubs, lavatories, and sinks and the wall or vertical support to which the tub or other receptacle is secured. The joint is adjustable in order to conform to the contour of the article to which the joint is applied as well as any irregularities in the surface of the wall. Patent was applied for Feb. 5, 1934, and issued Aug. 6, 1935.

without discontinuing any current, or even old, popular lines. After all, glassware, like clothing, was more sensitive to fashion trends than bathtubs.

Yet the appearance of Sakier's tubs was a significant selling point. As Director of the Bureau of Design Development for the American Radiator Standard Sanitary Corporation, Sakier invented mechanical devices to enable efficient installation and operation. However, he was better known for designing aesthetically pleasing modern streamlined forms. One of his most popular items was the Neo-Classic tub, pictured in contemporary periodicals and exhibited along with examples of other modern industrial design.

The name Neo-Classic, which he registered in 1929, did not at all refer to Classical Revival; it was intended to be taken literally as "new classic." New classicism was based on geometry associated with the new machinery. Automobiles and airplanes seemed to require straight lines and symmetry. There was no place in a modern society, according to Sakier, for "vaporous spirals and meaningless curves" which had been formerly used on anything from subway entrances to beds. Although he did not call it by name, Sakier obviously did not care for Art Nouveau. Rather than "new art" he referred to the Art Nouveau style as "Victorian elaboration at its zenith."[15]

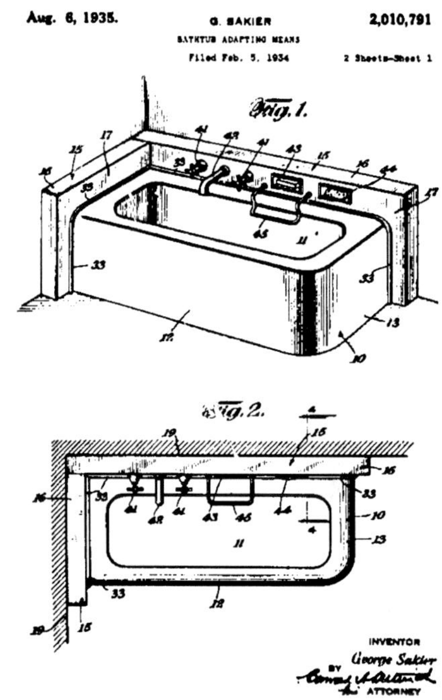

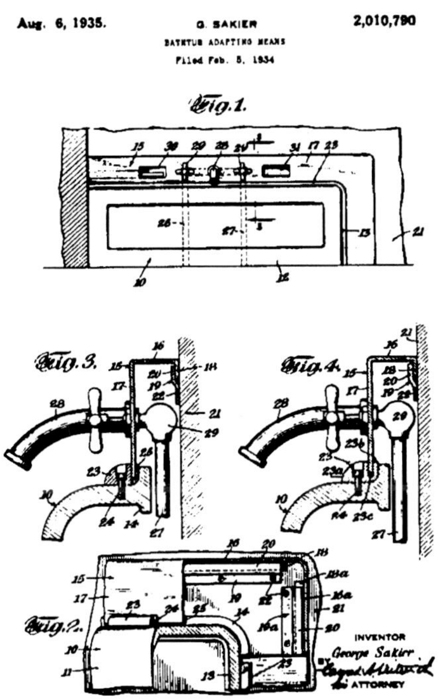

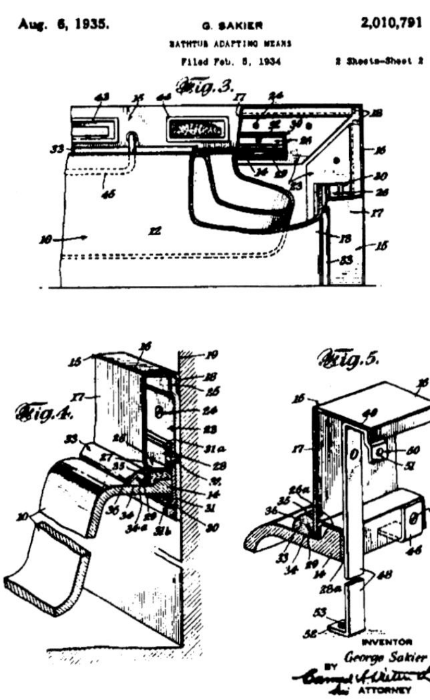

3.4, 3.5, 3.6. Patent drawing of bathtub adapting means: provides simple, efficient, and inexpensive means by which old bathtubs on legs or feet can be replaced with a modern "apron" type without tearing out the old piping or damaging bathroom walls or floors. The new panel is designed to receive and conceal old piping and includes a new element to accommodate valves, spout, grab bar, soap and sponge receptacles, and an upper portion which can serve as a shelf for toilet articles. A water-tight joint is provided between the tub and adapting element. Patent was applied for Feb. 5, 1934, and issued Aug. 6, 1935.

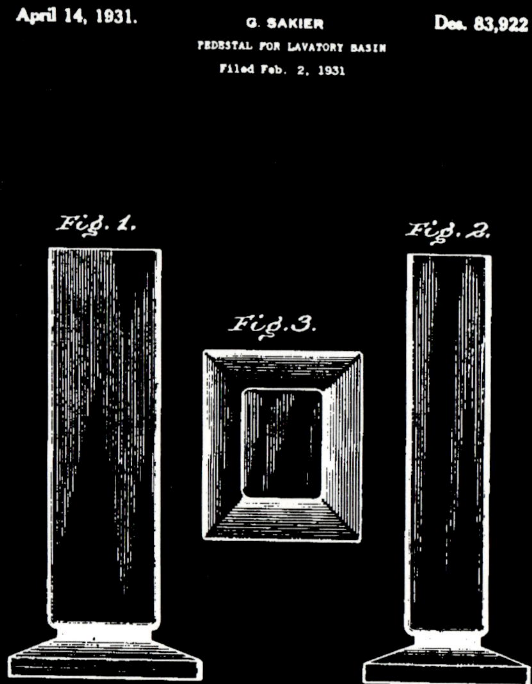

3.7 Pedestal design of lavatory basin for the Standard Sanitary Manufacturing Co., applied for Feb. 2, 1931, and issued April 14, 1931.

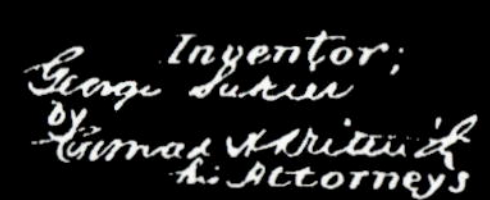

3.8 Patent drawing of tub design for the Standard Sanitary Manufacturing Co., applied for Nov. 6, 1930, and issued Sept. 8, 1931. This was pictured in the May 1934 issue of *Architectural Forum.*

According to Sakier, scientific forms were based on geometry; therefore, a new appreciation of geometric form became the essence of modern style. America, Sakier believed, was THE modern country and said: "We do not have to strive for modernity; we simply cannot help being modern."[16] He saw Europeans as trying to get away from the antique partly because they had seen so much of it and partly because they associated the un-modern inconveniences of their lives with the antique surroundings in which they lived. The new form of art, industrial design, was well suited to America; until its introduction, America had little to boast in the way of significant artistic originality. America's classics were being created as he spoke. Another modernist, William Lescaze, concurred: "We are the classicists of tomorrow and none of us doubts it." Sakier was considered a "pioneer leader among today's artists in industry." The principles of form, relationship, and expressiveness of materials found in his plumbing fixtures were compared to those of Constantin Brancusi's sculptures.[17]

CLOSURE NEWS

SAKIER: REALIST

If you want to throw out all the emotions, intangibles and aesthetic-twaddle from this industrial design business and get down to solid facts, go up to 40 East 40th St., N.Y.C., and talk to George Sakier. He'll tell you that "any industrial art is good if it makes people want the product."

Call it heresy, or cynicism, or what you will. The fact remains that it's the realistic viewpoint a designer gets when his entire present and future depends on sales results. As director of American Radiator and Standard Sanitary's design bureau, Sakier is too mature to indulge his private fancies and preferences, or to try "raising America's cultural standards." The fact that his bathroom fixture and accessory designs are sales successes, and are at the same time invariably beautiful, should give both idealists and cynics food for thought.

Despite the peculiar set-up of the sanitary industry, which precludes overnight revolutions, one can see real results of Sakier's work. America is fast becoming beautiful-bathroom-conscious. And no wonder. Sakier's bathroom designs and decorative schemes are extremely attractive, yet completely practical for average purses. Recently he designed the first complete factory-fabricated, ready-to-install bathroom unit, for both old and new buildings. Tiling, plastering, painting and carpentry are eliminated, and beautiful bathrooms replace dingy old ones almost miraculously and at low cost. His bureau really acts as a clearing house for information directly or indirectly affecting the aesthetic or structural design of sanitation, heating and ventilating units, and its files are consulted by architects, speculative builders, investment bankers, decorators and editors, for data on latest trends in decoration, materials, sales features, sanitary layout and so forth.

Sakier is a strange combination of artist-engineer-merchandiser. He was formerly art director for *Harper's Bazaar*, and for years he designed automatic machinery, and now much of his work concerns sales promotion. Recently the A. R. & S. S. World's Fair Exhibit came up for designing and layout, and Sakier's problem was to interest visitors already bored with too much machinery. Sakier planned a gentle outside ramp, leading visitors upstairs first, where a balcony overlooked the entire exhibit and faced a huge photomontage mural of famous A. R. & S. S. equipped buildings.

In addition to his work at American Radiator, Sakier is chief designer for Fostoria Glass. By way of showing his competence on small objects as well as large, we illustrate a couple of his Fostoria designs: a classically gorgeous urn and a short-stemmed goblet, distinguished by a delicate and buoyant all-over design. Both Sakier and Fostoria officials correctly and profitably aimed the latter at a fairly affluent stratum, only to discover that German and Czech glass factories were selling low-priced but accurate copies in American chain stores. The piracy, first in American industrial art industry, naturally annoyed Fostoria, but Sakier gets some comfort out of it. It seems to prove that design is vital to mass-market as well as class-market goods.

3.9 Magazine article picturing Sakier and his designs for sink, tub, faucet, and Fostoria glass. *Courtesy of the George Sakier Foundation.*

Some years after both Sakier and the president of American Standard Radiator had left the company, he wrote to Sakier. When Standard Sanitary merged with American Radiator (eventually becoming American Standard) Sakier had apparently found himself in the middle of some executive rivalry. A vice president of Standard Sanitary by the name of Reed even made comments to Sakier such as: "If you did something good, I would not like it." Nevertheless, Reed did approve Sakier's designs and the company enjoyed the resultant profits. In another story, Sakier was clearly the hero. Theo Arens, president of American Radiator, wanted the contract for the new and very prestigious Waldorf Astoria hotel so badly he could taste it. The architect, Theo Schultz, of the firm Schultz and Weaver, was leaning toward Kohler plumbing fixtures just like the ones his firm had used in the newly completed Pierre Hotel. Arens told Sakier to design a new line of fixtures for American Radiator in order to compete for the coveted Waldorf Astoria contract. His Neo-Classic design duly impressed Schultz, won the contract, and added to Sakier's growing reputation, not to mention doubling his annual salary. Several of Sakier's contemporaries praised the design: Architect Raymond Hood called the Neo-Classic fixtures "very interesting from an architect's point of view...they have an architectural character

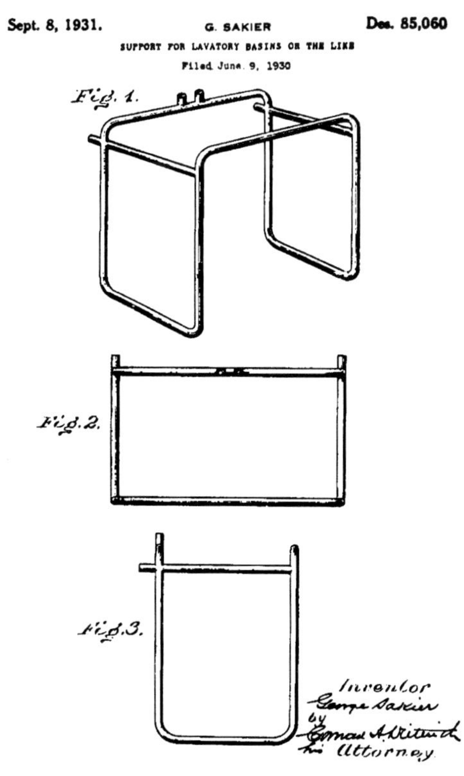

3.10 Patent drawing of tubular support for lavatory basin, applied for June 9, 1930, and received Sept. 8, 1931.

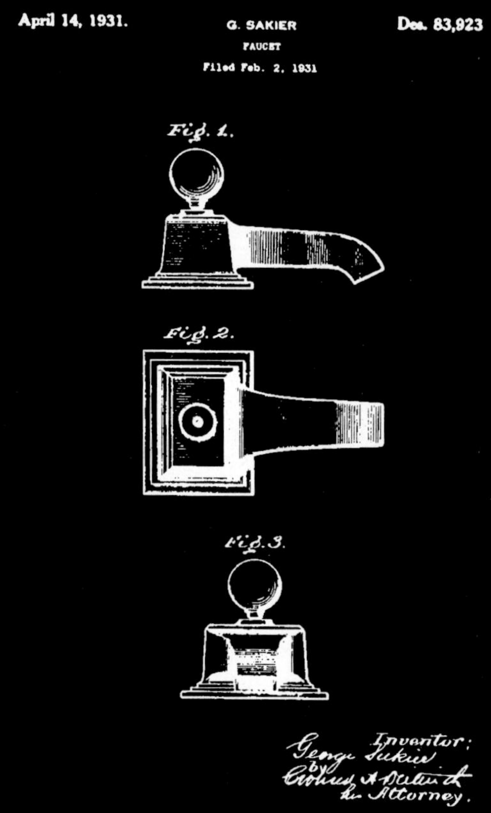

3.11 Patent drawing of Neo-Classic faucet design for the Standard Sanitary Manufacturing Co., applied for Feb. 2, 1931, and issued April 14, 1931. This was pictured in the May 1934 issue of *Architectural Forum.*

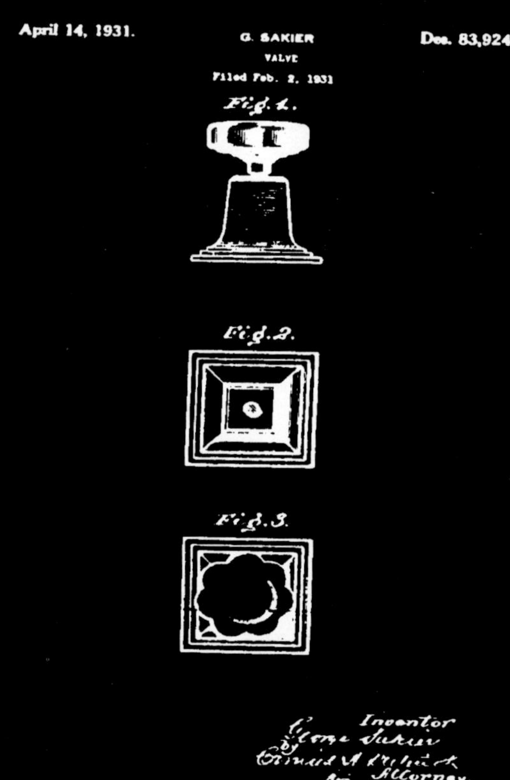

3.12 Patent drawing of valve design, applied for Feb. 2, 1931, and issued April 14, 1931.

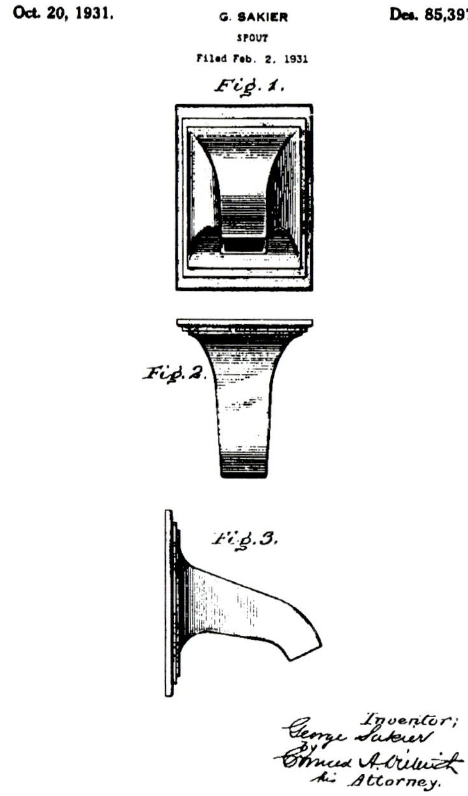

3.13 Patent drawing of spout design, applied for Feb. 2, 1931, and issued Oct. 20, 1931.

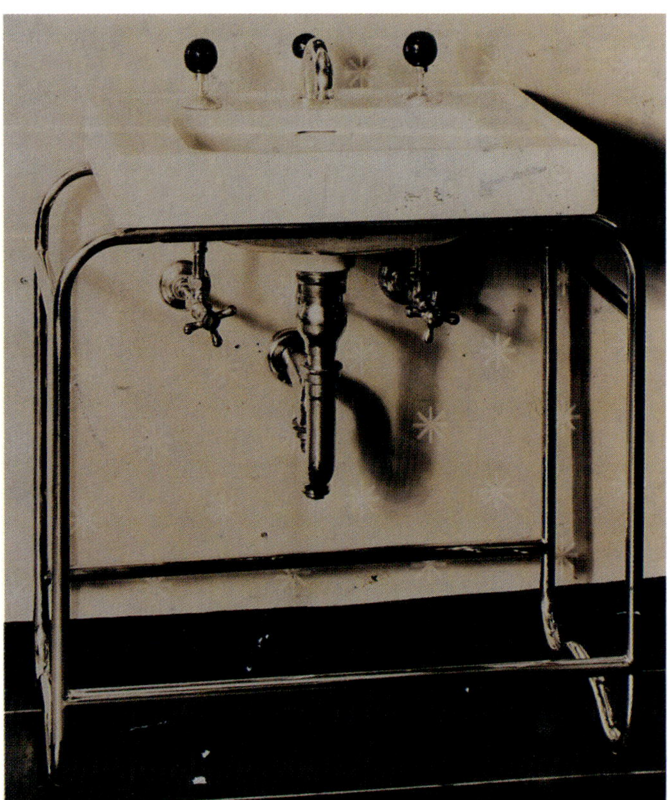

3.14 Sink design with black porcelain knobs and chromium plated faucet with patented tubular sink support (filed June 9, 1930). *Courtesy of the George Sakier Foundation.*

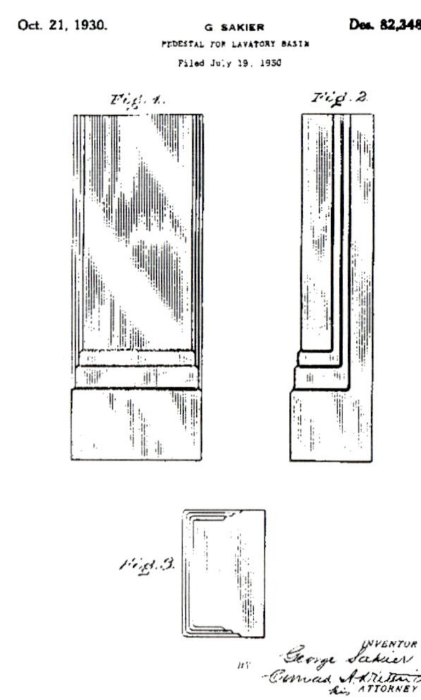

3.15 Patent drawing of pedestal for lavatory basin designed for the Waldorf Astoria hotel, applied for July 19, 1930, and issued Oct. 21, 1930.

that blends them into the design of the room. They have the basic qualities of good design, of being straightforward and simple." *House and Garden* editor Richardson Wright said that the fixtures "excite my interest beyond their beauty...Sakier has extracted the full significance of the modern movement and brought to it a balance and maturity which gives modern design, for the first time, the character and stability of a normal period." (I wonder what he meant by "normal" period.) Industrial designer Joseph Platt described the fixtures as having "captured in their splendid simplicity the very best culled from the last few years' experience in the modern movements. They point a way for future domestic design and have that quality of agelessness which could render them ideal for the moment and lovely for all time."[18]

On the heels of success followed the complex issue of design piracy. To a designer, imitation was a form of flattery. Sakier said that "there are more unsung triumphs of industrial design in Woolworth's than elsewhere" and he felt elated when he saw copies of his designs at variety chains.[19] (Apparently he was not working on a royalty basis.) To a manufacturer, however, copying carried very negative financial implications. In a 1931 letter to Sakier, the first vice president of American Standard Sanitary, Theo E. Mueller, expressed his anxiety over a wave of design piracy. At the time of the letter, they had not yet received the patent that Sakier had applied for fourteen months earlier. It wasn't until the following year that he was finally granted the patent on the Neo-Classic tub.

3.16 Photo of popular design for chromium plated lavatory fittings with black porcelain knobs, as it appeared in numerous publications including *Arts and Decoration* in 1935, *Yearbook of the Architectural League of New York* in 1933, and *Studio Yearbook* of 1935. *Courtesy of the George Sakier Foundation.*

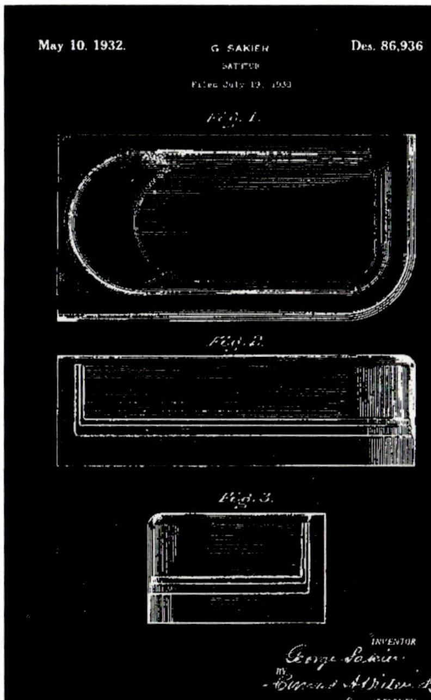

3.17 Patent drawing of Neo-Classic bathtub, applied for July 19, 1930, and issued May 10, 1932.

Since Sakier also dabbled in interior design, he did not limit himself to the plumbing fixtures in the bathroom. He looked at the room as a whole, combining the selection of colors and materials and the arrangement of objects (what interior decorators did) with new designs for functional items (industrial design) with their proper installation and aesthetically pleasing integration into existing architecture (interior design). His bathroom creations featured in periodicals and exhibits had porcelain or enamelled metal fixtures in colors like malachite green, delicate pink, coral red, and soft purplish-grey. He favored tinted mirrors, painted or marbleized walls, and water-resist wallpapers. Sakier must have had great fun working with mirrors. The walls of more than one of his bathrooms were entirely covered with mirrors with grey or gun metal backing and upper panels with etched coral and other undersea motifs. A full-length dressing mirror and a smaller mirror were illuminated by lamps which were concealed behind narrow panels of frosted glass. His Adapto bathtub was designed to accommodate either a tiled front or a fixed center panel of glass or wood with cupboards concealed by side panels.[20]

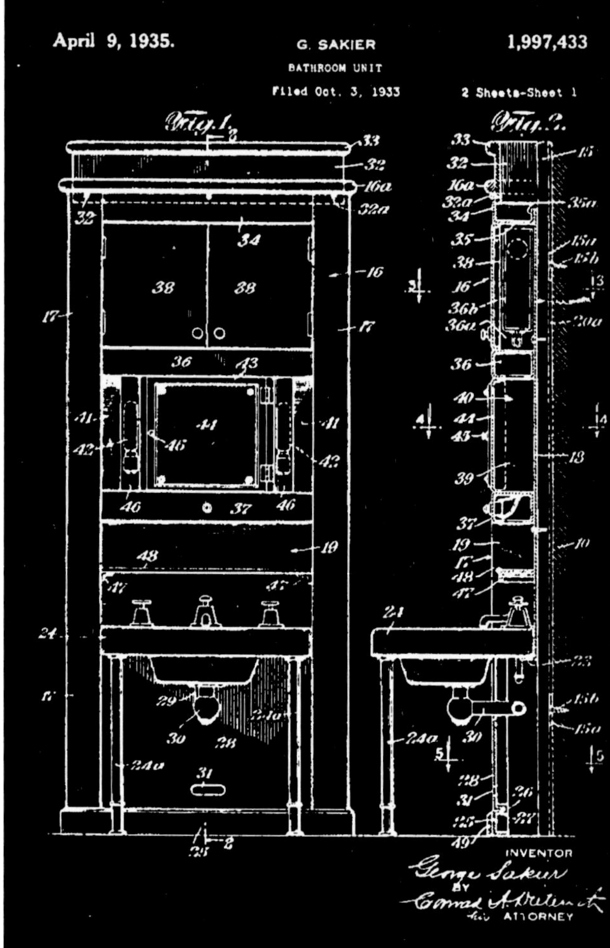

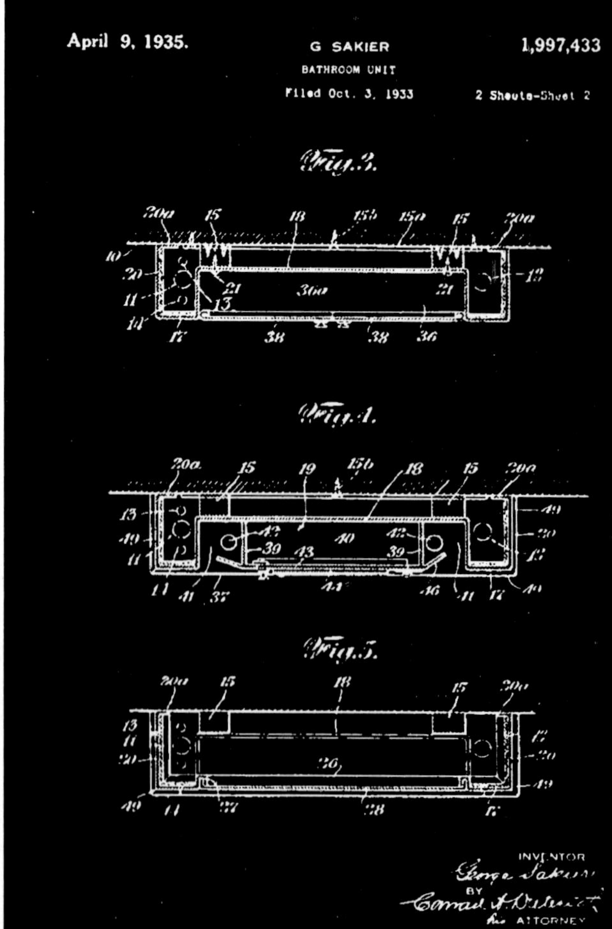

3.18 & 3.19 Patent drawing for Arco Unit Panel System, a prefabricated bathroom panel for the Accessories Company intended to modernize an older bathroom without tearing out the old rough plumbing. By making the new casing in two telescoping parts it can be adjusted to fit rooms of different heights. In addition to covering water supply, soil, and vent pipes, the panel receives and partly supports the sink and accommodates a medicine cabinet, shelves, lights, etc. The design also enables ready access to concealed plumbing for inspection or repair. Since each unit forms a competed wall section and provides the complete working elements of the bathroom, it is suitable for new construction as well as remodeling.

In order to eliminate the need for unnecessary steps as well as design professions, Sakier developed the prefabricated bathroom. Not the mirrored-walled novelties to amuse the upper classes, these were intended to aid a building industry unable to provide sufficient low-cost housing. American Radiator sought a partial solution to the housing dilemma with prefabricated bathrooms stamped from metal. In fact, they were the first prefabricated housing units actually produced, but not without problems: when the first prefabricated house with Sakier's prefabricated bathroom was unveiled by Eleanor Roosevelt, it was boycotted by the plumber's union.

Sakier and others believed that the trend in both housing construction and interior decoration was toward the increased use of prefabrication. Regarding the interior, he wrote, "Prefabrication should hold great interest for interior decorators for they can introduce as much or as little of it in their work as they desire. It eliminates, for instance, all the mechanical problems in a bathroom and makes it a purely decorative problem."[21] He patented the Arco Unit Panel System (see drawing) for the Accessories Company, a division of American Radiator Company. Each unit formed a complete wall section and supplied the total working elements of the bathroom. It was not only appropriate for new construction but for the modernization of older bathrooms without necessitating the removal of any existing rough plumbing. By making the new casing in two telescoping parts, a unit could be adjusted to fit rooms of varying heights. Besides covering water supply, soil, and vent pipes, the panel would receive and partly support the sink as well as accommodate a medicine cabinet, shelves, lights, etc. The design also enabled ready access to concealed plumbing for inspection or repair.

A complete bathroom with its three major fixtures plus prefabricated walls, ceilings, and floors, also made by the Accessories Company, could be assembled as a single unit, or the parts could be used separately. In 1934 there were 133 of these units installed in a Washington, D. C., apartment building, and another 400 had already been specified for another building. By the next year, thousands of the prefabricated bathroom units were in use in homes and apartment buildings.[22] The Accessories Company was confident that the product would continue to sell on its own merit; their decision to provide neither displays nor advertising proved to be a very bad idea. When a series of more elaborate units were featured in the 1936 *Studio Yearbook*, the focus was more on Sakier's modern novelties than on the issue of prefabrication.

Prefabrication and the bath

AMONG the new tendencies seen in bathrooms is a system of prefabricated panels, each containing a unit of equipment ready to install. A number of these units comprise the finished room. The system was designed by George Sakier for The Accessories Company, Inc., division of American Radiator Company. This room is further described in the text

3.20 Prefabrication and the bath as it appeared in *House and Garden* in 1935. Caption reads: "Among the new tendencies seen in bathrooms is a system of prefabricated panels, each containing a unit of equipment ready to install. A number of these units comprise the finished room. The system was designed by George Sakier for The Accessories Company Inc. a division of American Radiator Company." *Copyright 1935 (renewed 1963) by the Condé Nast Publications Inc., photo courtesy House and Garden.*

Of special note were a mirrored door, mirrors set in the wall paneling, a bathtub set into a separate alcove with independent lighting, a vertically-positioned handrail by the tub, protective railing to keep items from sliding off the shelf along the tub, and a pneumatic cushion head rest. There were other clever items with both functional and decorative appeal: a chromium-plated towel basket, a scale that was flush with the floor with the dial completely separate and framed on the wall, a large built-in cabinet with glass shelves and sliding glass doors that were flush with the wall, Neo-Classic pedestal sink, and a sheet-glass table with a wooden frame. Another of Sakier's table designs was featured in *House Furnishing Review* in 1933. This dressing table was 32 inches wide and 16 1/2 inches deep with a frame of triple chromium-plated steel tubing. The heavily-lacquered metal drawers had removable linings for easy cleaning. A shelf was wood veneered in metal, and the table top was plate glass to keep the cosmetics in sight. The accompanying wall mirror concealed the lighting equipment, and a reflector threw the light through a sandblasted border on the mirror. A stool with tubular steel frame came with the table.[23] Another of his bathroom conveniences was a shadowless shaving mirror built into the medicine cabinet.

3.21 Three prefabricated units: each major plumbing element is delivered with its wall section ready for installation in various combinations.

Somewhere in this array of high-style designer gadgets the original and noble plan to service a large segment of the population with a low-cost "machine for cleanliness" based on the idea of prefabrication was lost. Where the Accessories Company failed to adequately market the economical and practical stamped metal units, at least the decorative arts journals pictured them. Ironically, these units were so upstaged by wonderfully glitzy decorations and accessories that they were barely noticed.

The kitchen was another place in which Sakier could combine plumbing innovation with modern styling. With almost Wrightian enthusiasm (or ego) for total design, Sakier could not stop at the plumbing. His Arcode kitchen unit system was made completely of metal, with the exception of Formica counter tops and linoleum flooring. Even the trim was an aluminum alloy. Color schemes, in the most modern taste, might combine grey, ivory, chartreuse, and vermillion.

In 1935 and 1936 issues of *House & Garden*, Sakier presented some of his energy-saving devices for the kitchen: a meat grinder ledge attachment that allowed the grinder to be securely fastened wherever the food was being prepared; a fold-down breadboard that rested firmly on the worktop with a rack to hang knives in the recessed compartment behind the stored board; a cup rack attached to the underside of shelves; a dashboard with electrical outlets and switches for small appliances; a mixer garage with a place for accessories in the cabinet directly above it; a recessed towel hanger at the sink; a wire rack, hung above the drain board next to the sink, to provide added space for wet dishes; a kitchen office for papers with a place for cookbooks; a food preparation cabinet; and a do-it-yourself utility table on wheels. Storage cabinets in Sakier's kitchens came in standard depths of 6 1/2, 13, or 21 inches and could be readily assembled in combinations to any length or configuration. Cabinet doors came solid or of glass framed in polished chromium. Drawers were available in three sizes and were designed to slide smoothly and noiselessly. Sakier even provided a method of installing this kitchen to insure that doors hung plumb, straight, and firmly, and the drawers did not stick.[24] Such kitchen conveniences were far from being frivolous or trendy. Sakier had undoubtedly cooked and had used a kitchen. He was, however, at no loss for decorative treatments and specified that cabinets should be of enameled steel; serving tables should be of chromium tubing with linoleum tops, metal chairs should be upholstered in lacquered fabric, and the linoleum flooring should be inlaid with contrasting patterns.

Whether designing bathrooms and kitchens because of his interest in plumbing fixtures, or living rooms because he enjoyed color, texture, and pattern, Sakier worked with the current vocabulary of modern design. His use of mirrors, metals, and high-contrast color schemes was not unlike the work of his peers in New York and European style centers. Early in his interior design career, however, Sakier, like so many of his contemporaries, also worked in a more traditional mode. In an article with sections entitled "Interiors by the Yard" and "Effects in Plastic Pulp," Sakier's interior renderings depicted period styles. Neoclassical was not yet Neo-Classic. His designs for decorative pendants, plaques, moldings, friezes, dados, and ceilings were executed in "plastic pulp" that had been molded between engraved steel plates and imported by W. H. S. Lloyd & Company. They were used in rooms with marbleized walls and gold stars and buttons in relief.[25]

Left: 3.23 Table exhibited at the Brooklyn Museum with cylindrical vases that were exhibited at the Museum of Modern Art, 1930s. *Courtesy of the George Sakier Foundation.*

Below: 3.24 Sakier's apartment on East 57th Street in New York: both tables are his designs. *Courtesy of the George Sakier Foundation.*

Above: 3.22 Sakier's New York apartment pictured in the 1935 *Studio Yearbook* with the title "A Modernized Living Room." The fireplace surround is faced with black slate; this was discovered when an ordinary stock mantel was removed. Floor-to-ceiling concave brass sheets form half-columns which flank the fireplace and reflect the light. The color scheme is neutral from whites to tans and beige. Glass jars in front of the fireplace were designed by Sakier. *Photo by Eugene Hutchinson, courtesy of the George Sakier Foundation.*

3.25 Sakier's New York studio. *Courtesy of the George Sakier Foundation.*

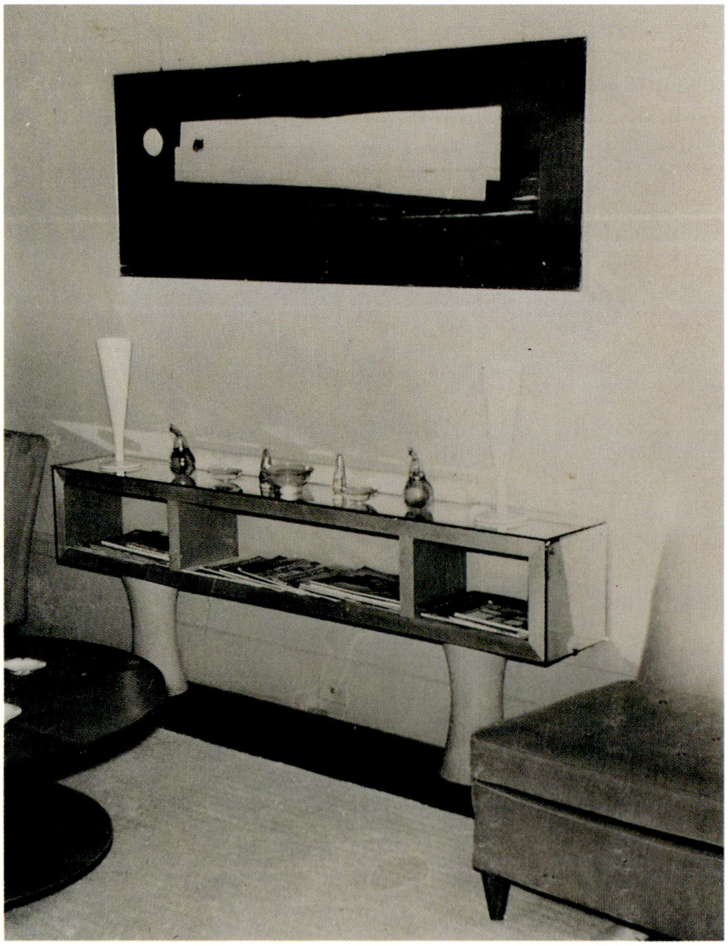

3.26 View of Sakier's studio as pictured in the article, "George Sakier: Artist and Machine Become Reconciled." *Courtesy of the George Sakier Foundation.*

Sakier was written about and wrote articles for *House & Garden*. Like the arbiters of taste once popular with Victorian audiences, Sakier took the opportunity to dictate some twentieth-century style. His guide for using black, grey, and white schemes throughout the house even specified furniture of light-colored wood that was to be stained grey. A lesson in another article took the form of a typology of fourteen different flooring materials and their uses.[26] Interior designs for his own apartments and homes were, for the most part, modern, but sometimes included a few Neoclassical elements. Despite his understanding of and appreciation for new materials and methods, Sakier also recognized the need for some traditional components, and wrote, "Mankind has a certain affinity for certain types of materials — an affinity which exists deep in the consciousness. Only when price is predominant are substitutes accepted...Machine-made furniture of today cannot [become] heirlooms of the future because it lacks human warmth and frailty."[27] In 1935 his own dining room was described as being a combination of period and modern: the walls and satin upholstery of Louis XVI style dining chairs were in an apricot color; the rug under the table was bright red; the dining table had a gold mirrored top supported by two cast iron café table pedestals; a built-in buffet was made of waxed "presdwood" with mirror-backed niches for display.[28] Obviously Sakier's fascination with mirrors went beyond the bathroom. In fact, his interest in interior design extended to ultimately include the whole building, and he designed two houses on Long Island and one in France.

3.27 Another of Sakier's house designs. *Courtesy of the George Sakier Foundation.*

3.28 House in Bridgehampton, Long Island designed by Sakier. *Courtesy of the George Sakier Foundation.*

3.29 Sakier standing in front of one of his Long Island homes. *Courtesy of the George Sakier Foundation.*

3.30 Long Island home before the arches were added to the porch. *Courtesy of the George Sakier Foundation.*

In the midst of this multi-dimensional career, Sakier lightly described himself as "the plumber who won a national competition for a whiskey label."[29] Rather than pretending to be modest, he was really expressing the ease with which he could travel between two and three-dimensional design. The whiskey label was for Schenley Products Company in New York. His contract with the company as Art Director began June 14, 1934 and included "the necessary cooperation with Advertising and Production and Sales Departments." An annual salary of $15,000 for the first year was to rise to $20,000 in the second year.[30]

Below Left: 3.31 Sakier's designs for Schenley: left, Old Schenley Rye packaging; top right, Old Schenley Rye in display carton, packed one to every case; bottom right, counter display for miniatures, one of which was packed in every case of miniatures. *All product packaging and photos courtesy of the George Sakier Foundation.*

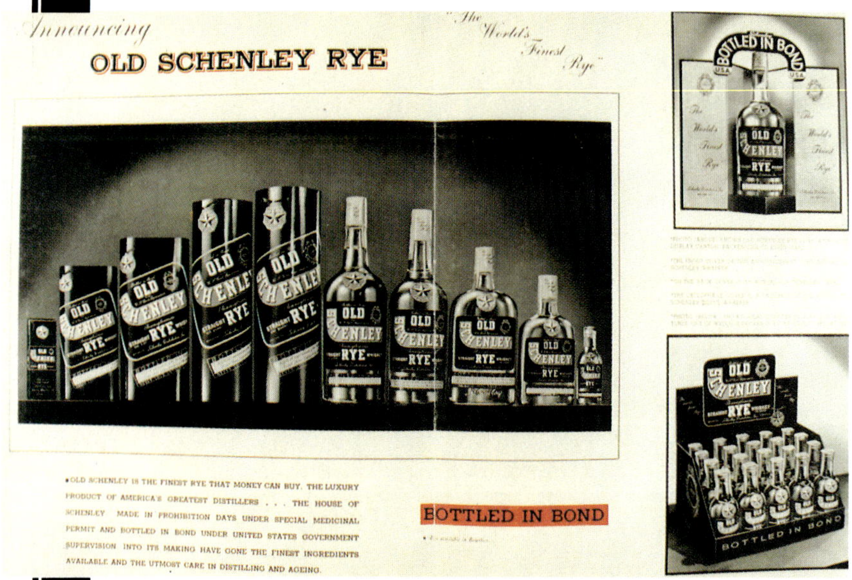

3.33 Back cover of Schenley brochure with actual label.

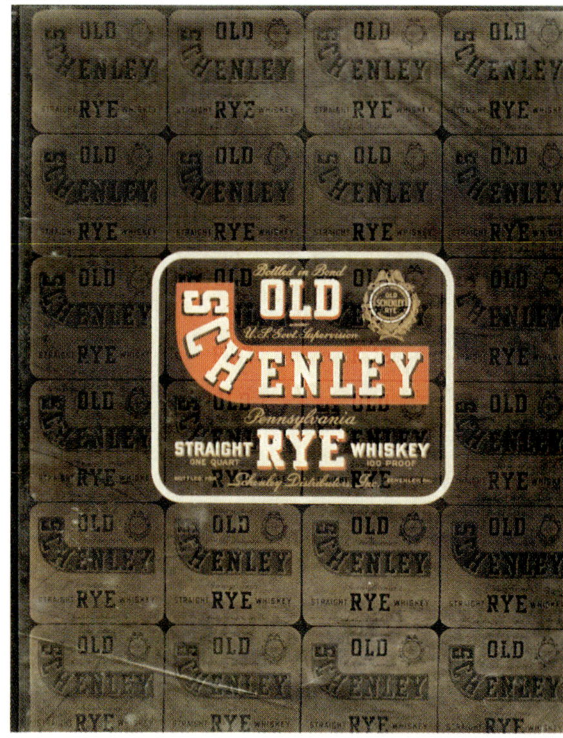

3.32 Front cover of Old Schenley promotional brochure with actual label; the cellophane cover is a facsimile of the original tissue wrapper.

3.34 Old Schenley tissue wrapper from promotional brochure.

3.36 Schenley's Mayflower Rye packaging.

3.35 Schenley whiskey packaging.

Above and Right: 3.37 Old Schenley Rye labels.

3.38 Schenley's Mayflower Rye label.

3.39 American Management Association award for Sakier's Old Schenley packaging design, 1935.

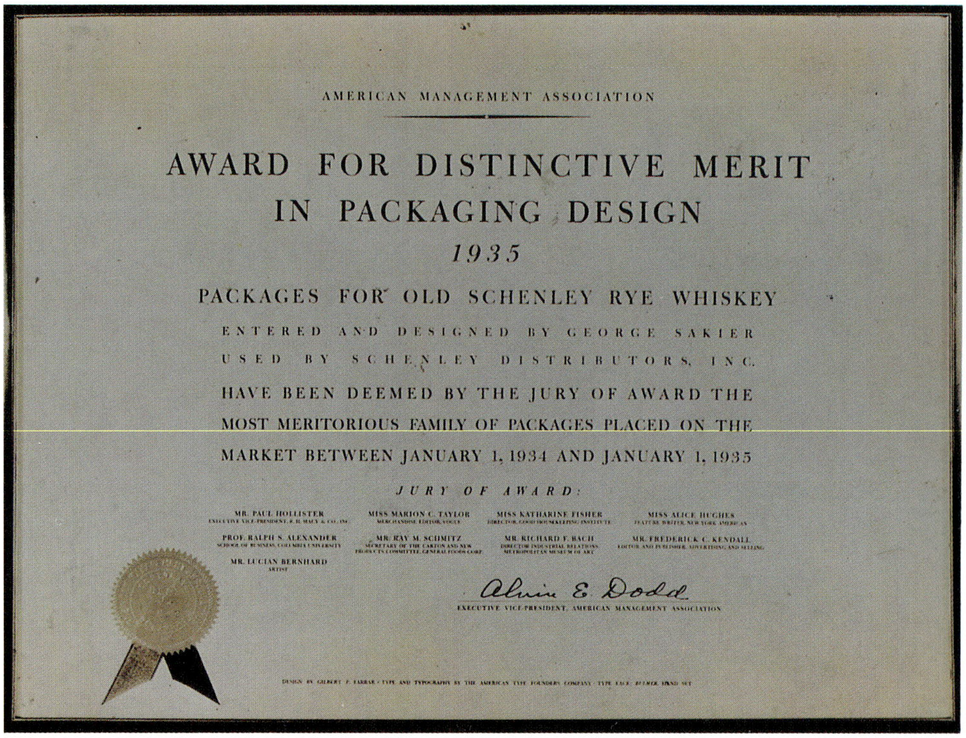

AMERICAN MANAGEMENT ASSOCIATION

AWARD FOR DISTINCTIVE MERIT
IN PACKAGING DESIGN
1935

PACKAGES FOR OLD SCHENLEY RYE WHISKEY
ENTERED AND DESIGNED BY GEORGE SAKIER
USED BY SCHENLEY DISTRIBUTORS, INC.
HAVE BEEN DEEMED BY THE JURY OF AWARD THE
MOST MERITORIOUS FAMILY OF PACKAGES PLACED ON THE
MARKET BETWEEN JANUARY 1, 1934 AND JANUARY 1, 1935

JURY OF AWARD:

MR. PAUL HOLLISTER, EXECUTIVE VICE-PRESIDENT, R. H. MACY & CO., INC.
MISS MARION C. TAYLOR, MERCHANDISE EDITOR, VOGUE
MISS KATHARINE FISHER, DIRECTOR, GOOD HOUSEKEEPING INSTITUTE
MISS ALICE HUGHES, FEATURE WRITER, NEW YORK AMERICAN
PROF. RALPH S. ALEXANDER, SCHOOL OF BUSINESS, COLUMBIA UNIVERSITY
MR. RAY M. SCHMITZ, SECRETARY OF THE CARTON AND NEW PRODUCTS COMMITTEE, GENERAL FOODS CORP.
MR. RICHARD F. BACH, DIRECTOR INDUSTRIAL RELATIONS, METROPOLITAN MUSEUM OF ART
MR. FREDERICK C. KENDALL, EDITOR AND PUBLISHER, ADVERTISING AND SELLING
MR. LUCIAN BERNHARD, ARTIST

Alvin E. Dodd
EXECUTIVE VICE-PRESIDENT, AMERICAN MANAGEMENT ASSOCIATION

DESIGN BY GILBERT P. FARRAR · TYPE AND TYPOGRAPHY BY THE AMERICAN TYPE FOUNDERS COMPANY · TYPE FACE: BULMER HAND SET

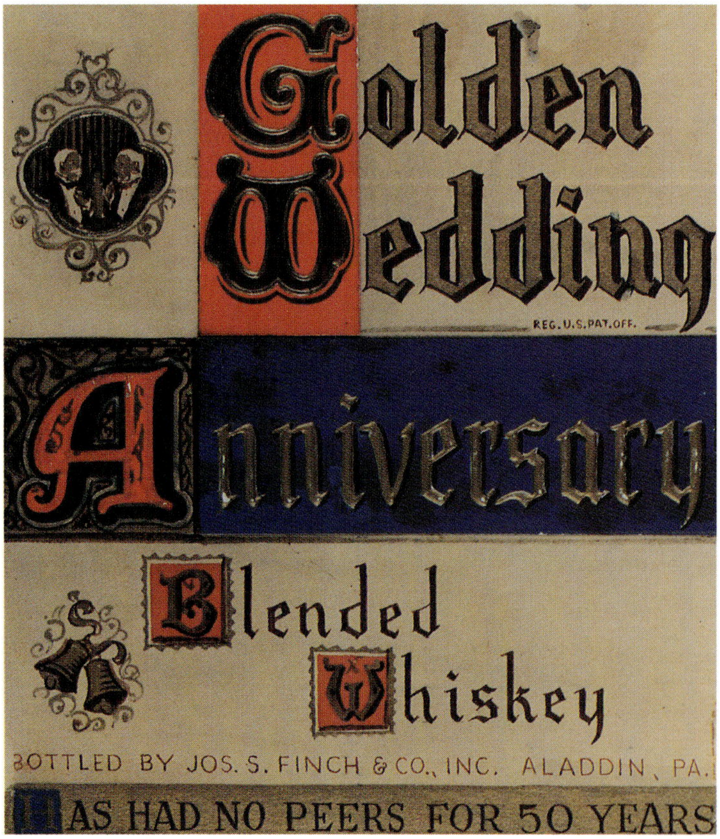

3.41 Slightly different version of Golden Wedding Anniversary label.

3.40 Golden Wedding Anniversary label.

3.42 Three Feathers Gin label.

3.43 Slightly different version of Three Feathers Gin label.

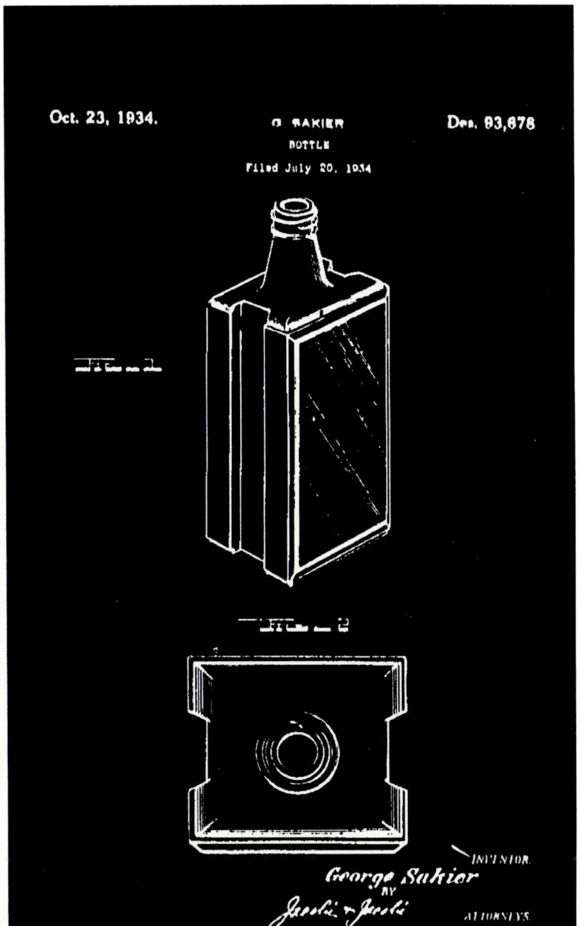

3.44 Patent drawing of bottle design for Schenley Products Co. showing perspective view and top view, applied for July 20, 1934, and received Oct. 34, 1934.

Another award for product packaging design came in1943 for his Escape Perfume package for Mary Dunhill Inc. In a letter dated Feb. 4, 1944, Dunhill executive vice-president Arthur Mainzer thanked Sakier for his design that won the 1943 packaging award of "Beauty Fashion Magazine." He also designed packaging for Alfred Dunhill Men's Toiletries, Ltd. Examples illustrated in the Society of Industrial Designers 1951 yearbook were described as, "bottles, made on fully automatic machines, have Durez plastic caps with lacquered brass inserts. The gold-embossed label and the carton are simulated fine grain leather."[31]

Grover A. Whalen of Schenley Products was president of the World's Fair Corporation and a speaker at the inaugural ceremonies of the 1939 New York World's Fair.[32] He may also have influenced the Fair committee's decision to invite Sakier to design the Science and Education focal exhibits at the fair. (Coincidentally, Sakier's award for the Schenley logo was also in 1939.) Since both science and education held considerable interest for Sakier (not to mention the prestige accorded the project), he accepted with enthusiasm. The advisory committee on Science, chaired by Dr. Albert Einstein, who was then with the Princeton University school of Graduate Studies, represented a range of interests. For example, Dr. Frank Jewett, vice president of A.T. & T., represented industry; Dr. Karl Compton, president of M.I.T., represented physics; Paul Mann of Evander Childs High School represented children's interests; Waldeman Kaempffert, the *New York Times* science editor, represented the public; and several other prominent members of the science community represented fields such as engineering, research, chemisty, and biology.

3.45 Sakier's award-winning package design for Mary Dunhill "Escape."

3.47 Mary Dunhill "White Hyacinth Cologne" label.

3.46 Mary Dunhill cosmetic packaging.

3.48 Mary Dunhill White Hyacinth packaging.

3.49 Mary Dunhill "Bewitching" Dusting Powder packaging.

3.50 Mary Dunhill Bewitching Cologne packaging.

3.51 Photo used in Dunhill full-page magazine advertisements. In a handwritten note attached to an ad, Sakier wrote, "a classic after 30 years still best selling. Reflects my love for geometric form as a machine design."

3.52 Dunhill men's toiletries advertisement.

3.53 Alfred Dunhill Men's Toiletries Ltd., a similar photo was pictured in the Society of Industrial Designer's *1951 U. S. Industrial Design.*

3.54 Alfred Dunhill carton design for after shave.

The inscription for the Science and Education exhibit read, "Wings for Man; A Symbol of Human Aspirations." The exhibit, like its airplane theme, had two wings — one for Science and the other for education. On the main Science wall were seven large glass transparencies like "stained glass windows for a cathedral of science," painted by Allen Saalbury. Sakier explained, "I have tried to present the subject with human simplicity, in a spirit as broad as that conceived by the committee. To show that science is not merely machinery and test tubes, that education is not merely books and schools — to show that the two together constitute wings for man was my intention."[33] Running across the ceiling from the wall panels were seven brilliantly-colored channels pouring facts into a white reservoir; at eye level below were four frosted windows onto which slides were projected to illustrate the current advances of science and technology.

In the education wing, photomurals were mounted along one wall to illustrate the history of education from 1789 to the present 1939; a large mural was painted on the opposite wall. A series of thirty-two cartoon panels were displayed beneath the mural. These panels, which traced the education process from infancy to old age, were a collaborative effort of eleven leading American illustrators.

Both themes of science and education were focal. Dr. Gerald Wendt, the Fair's Director of Science and Education, explained: "The World's Fair as a whole is a vast exhibit of science. Nearly all of it has its education side. In accordance with its theme the Fair has made no effort to confine either science or education to a single building. It has, however...provided a great central exhibit on both subjects, which focuses the message of Science and Education for the World of Tomorrow."[34]

In addition to this important exhibit design, Sakier saw his bathrooms displayed at the Fair. One of these Art Deco rooms was described as having gunmetal mirrored walls with sandblasted motifs of marine vegetation, floors of turquoise, black, and white rubber, a pale turquoise ceiling, and Neo-Classic fixtures of shell-pink porcelain. One room had grey walls with white pilasters, marbleized panels, silver molding, a cream and black checkerboard floor made of rubber, and shiny black fixtures. Still another had an aquarium against a blue mirrored wall, white Sanitas wall covering with panels of deep blue glass, and a black linoleum floor.[35] The "World of Tomorrow" theme was right at home in Sakier's bathrooms.

Several industrial designers who had been responsible for exhibits at the 1939 World's Fair joined others in the field to found a professional organization in New York City in 1944. The new Society of Industrial Designers (SID) was chartered by fourteen leading design practitioners — Egmont Arens, Donald Desky, Norman Bel Geddes, Lurelle Guild, Raymond Loewy, Ray Patten, Joseph Platt, John Gordon Rideout, George Sakier, Jo Sinel, Brooks Stevens, Walter Dorwin Teague, Harold Van Doren, and Russel Wright. The first annual meeting was held on August 20, 1944, with Teague president, Dreyfuss vice-president, Loewy chairman of the executive committee, Van Doren treasurer, and Arens secretary.[36]

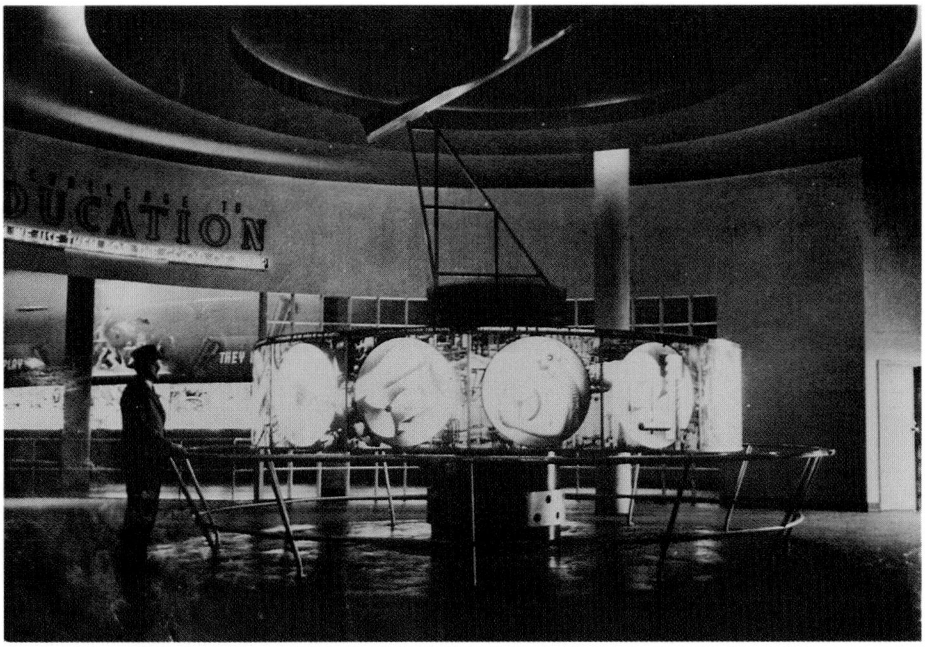

3.55 View of Sakier's Science and Education focal exhibit at the 1939 New York World's Fair.

It was an elite club. Charter member Brooks Stevens said, "I remember vividly the feeling of pride I had in being invited to join the gods on Mount Olympus at the first meeting in New York."[37] Mount Olympus was the right metaphor, especially if parallel lines and other clichés of streamlining are equated with fluting and other elements of classicism. Qualifications for membership were specific:

> Membership in the Society shall be limited to practicing Industrial Designers, and members of Industrial Design departments in institutions of higher learning...A candidate must have practiced Industrial Design for several years...must have had three or more of his products manufactured and offered for sale in the usual marketing channels. He must have honorably and satisfactorily served three or more manufacturers...The term Industrial Designer is defined to include persons who are professionally engaged in designing a diversity of products for machine and mass production.[38]

Richard F. Bach, dean of education at the Metropolitan Museum of Art, was a motivating force behind industrial arts and design exhibits at the museum. He held conferences in 1944 and 1946, which Sakier and several other SID members attended. As a result, they held an SID meeting in 1946 to discuss design education, which members felt was inadequate in the United States, especially in the areas of science and technology. In February 1947, SID announced a program of evening classes in collaboration with New York University; it was open to both designers and other interested students. The SID position on education was not to propose a model program, but to offer advice and support to those who asked for it. Sakier had long believed in providing advice and support, and he served on the Advisory Council of the Laboratory School of Industrial Design in New York City. The school was chartered by the New York State Board of Regents in 1937 after Federal support under the Federal Art project ran out. It offered a four-year industrial design course taught by practicing designers. In 1947, when Henry Dreyfuss was president of SID, Sakier headed the education committee and stressed the importance of education as one of the society's responsibilities.[39]

Both SID and the field of industrial design evolved rapidly. According to authority Arthur Pulos, "Before the war [industrial designers] had been associated with and in many cases responsible to businessmen and merchandisers; now they were directed by scientists and engineers."[40] In 1955 the organization's name was changed to the American Society of Industrial Designers (ASID); in 1965, as a result of a merger between several professional organizations, it became the Industrial Designers Society of America (IDSA). Sakier did not remain long enough to participate in these changes; although he was listed in the 1954 annual as having SID fellow status with an office at 159 East 69th Street in New York, by about 1950 he had already completed that chapter of his career. Like many expatriate artists before him, Sakier left the United States while retaining his citizenship. Settling in Paris to spend the second half of his life painting, he did not simply take an early retirement with a hobby; Sakier painted with dedication and passion. Yet, little is known about those years or the reasons for the change.

Chapter Four: Painting

As some writers are able to paint with words, some artists can create poetry with paint. Sakier aspired to paint poetry, and he dedicated most of his life to the quest. Knowing very early that a serious painter needs time to develop, he first followed other paths in order to earn the time needed to paint in comfort.

In many respects there were no better years to have practiced industrial design in the United States than in the late 1920s and the 1930s; the profession was brand new then, and the opportunities were waiting for those with imagination. While the field was still defining itself, packaging design and production glass design shared the industrial design umbrella. Sakier was widely recognized for designs of American Standard bathrooms, Schenley and Dunhill packaging, and Fostoria glass; but the reward that mattered most and enabled him to devote half of his life exclusively to painting was monetary. Without the substantial salaries and royalties from industrial design, Sakier would not have had the luxury of being able to maintain studios in Paris, Long Island, and Manhattan. In a 1970 exhibit brochure Sakier described some of his work as being from "the long period (1930 to 1940)," a time during which he practiced industrial design "to survive and achieve eventual independence."[1]

With few exceptions, all of Sakier's paintings (whether from the long period or after 1950 when he had achieved independence and could paint full-time) depict only two subjects — couples or landscapes. He also worked in essentially two styles — what he called realistic and abstract — though even his so-called realistic studies of nudes and of scenes have a distinctly abstract quality. Sakier even commented, "the realistic subjects have a definite abstract structure," and added, "all of my work whether abstract, imaginative, or realistic has been totally a celebration of my awe and delight in the mystery and beauty of nature."[2] It is no wonder then that Sakier's abstract landscapes seemed to combine the horizontality, radiance, and serenity of nineteenth-century American Luminism and the flat angular pattern of Japanese origami.

The realistic landscapes appear as if they were done in preparation for the abstractions, yet there does not seem to be any clear chronological sequence. Rather than a realistic period followed by an abstract period, Sakier's paintings were alternately realistic and abstract over the years. In fact, similar images in identical styles were sometimes painted decades apart, while completely different styles were used in the same year. Sakier explained, "In these realistic landscapes, I have made no attempt to interpret or to express myself — painting simply what I saw and felt — to absorb and understand. Any abstract content could be the unconscious choice of a pattern or motif and the inherent exclusion or emphasis to maintain it."[3] However, artist Ross Neher suggests that the decisive influence on Sakier's Realistic Landscapes of the 1940s was Surrealism. This was the time when Sakier painted many of his Realistic Landscapes and also when "Surrealism's influence on painting was at its apogee."[4]

Although Sakier was certainly aware of new art movements through his friendships and associations with leading artists in the United States and abroad, attributing influence can be tricky. He shared friendship with Hans and Sophie Arp but not artistic style. Arp's biomorphism was the antithesis of the angular forms that dominated Sakier's abstractions. Nor did Sakier's summer of 1922 in Austria with the Dadaists influence his work; he made it very clear that he was in no way part of that movement.[5]

At ease with the concepts of design, Sakier not only moved freely among the various industrial design fields, he made dimensional leaps between industry and fine art. He described his early work of the 1920s as being influenced by Kandinsky and Klee rather than Picasso's Cubism and called it "adventures in 'pure' form and color plus, hopefully, some poetry. Each is an encounter with a constellation of colors, and the emergence of the forms that most fulfill its meaning — but always an expression of what I seek and find in nature."[6]

No matter how abstract or minimal Sakier's images became, he never lost touch with nature. Even his imaginative paintings depicted nature, especially landscapes. "They are not specific memories," he explained, "but draw upon a distillation of many memories...are vehicles for totally abstract adventures in form and color."[7] He had often refered to form and color as being the essence of his career. Neher suggests that Sakier "predates Minimalism with his reduction of form to its essence." This was especially evident in his Abstract Couples, which Neher calls "Sakier's most poetic contribution to painting."[8] Earlier, another critic wrote, "and now he lives in Paris painting little lyrical miracles." This delighted Sakier, who responded, "contrary to the current [1970] ubiquitous love affair with frustration and futility, I believe stubbornly in the pleasure principle, and that to enjoy is to understand."[9] The following examples of Sakier's work, spanning seven decades, are presented here for just that — enjoyment. I believe that would have pleased Sakier.

4.1 New York landscape with buildings in the background, painted at age 17, signed and dated 1914. *All of the paintings shown are courtesy of the George Sakier Foundation.*

4.2 Study for realistic couple, 8 1/4 by 5 1/2 in.

4.4 Beach scene of bathing and seated nudes and one standing figure, 10 by 5 in.

4.3 Study of relaxed nude, 8 1/2 by 3 in.

4.5 Street scene with couple walking, 7 1/2 by 4 3/4 in.

4.6 Path leading to back of building with dark standing figure, 6 1/4 by 4 3/4 in.

4.7 Long Island coastal landscape Realistic Landscape showing an influence of nineteenth-century Luminism, 16 by 22 in.

4.8 RL 008 Realistic Landscape[10] of the Hamptons, painted in 1947, oil on composition board, 20 1/2 by 27 in.

4.9 RL 023 Realistic Landscape of the Hamptons, painted in 1946, oil on sheet aluminum, 16 1/2 by 21 1/2 in.

4.10 RL 029 Realistic Landscape of the Hamptons, painted 1940, oil on composition board, 15 1/2 by 21 in.

4.11 RL 013 Realistic Landscape of the Hamptons, painted 1940, oil on composition board, 16 by 22 in.

4.12 RL 022 Realistic Landscape of the Hamptons, painted 1945, oil on sheet aluminum, 16 by 21 1/2 in.

4.13 RL 002 Realistic Landscape of Mexico, painted 1940, oil on canvas, 21 1/2 by 29 1/2 in.

4.14 Untitled but probably another Mexican landscape of 1940.

4.15 RL 001 Realistic Landscape, 1947, oil on aluminum, 16 by 20 in.

4.16 RL 007 Realistic Landscape, 1950, oil on masonite board, 15 1/2 by 21 1/2 in.

4.17 RL 009 Realistic Landscape, 1946, oil on aluminum, 16 by 22 in.

4.18 AL 018 Abstract Landscape, 1962, oil on linen, 32 by 43 1/2 in.

4.19 AL 23 Abstract Landscape, 1960, oil on paper glued to plexiglass, 4 1/2 by 9 3/4 in.

4.20 AL 40 Abstract Landscape, 1962, oil on linen, 39 1/4 by 68 in.

4.21 AL 37 Abstract Landscape, 1960, oil on linen, 23 1/2 by 36 1/4 in.

4.22 AL 007 Abstract Landscape, 1975, oil on linen, 34 by 30 in.

Above Left: 4.23 M 5 Still Life with apple and pear, oil on paper glued to plexiglass, 6 3/4 by 9 3/4 in.

Above: 4.24 M 6 Still Life of plant, oil on linen, 12 1/2 by 21 in.

Left: 4.25 M 8 Still Life of flowers in a striped vase, oil on linen.

4.26 AC 013 Abstract Couple, oil on canvas, 28 3/4 by 29 in. This was the front cover illustration of the announcement for the Pratt exhibit "George Sakier: Correspondences."

4.27 AC 022 Abstract Couple, 1986, oil on linen, 28 by 41 in.

4.28 AC 004 Abstract Couple, 1959, oil on linen, 25 1/2 by 36 1/2 in.

4.29 AC 021 Abstract Couple, 1930, oil on linen, 25 by 38 1/2 in.

4.30 AC 019 Abstract Couple, 1940, oil on canvas.

4.31 AC 024 Abstract Couple, date uncertain — signed "Sakier 30" at bottom right and "Sakier 60" on the back, oil on linen, 34 by 52 1/2 in.

4.32 AC 001 Abstract Couple, 1930, oil on linen, 26 1/2 by 36 in.

4.33 AC 002 Abstract Couple, 1940, oil on linen, 26 1/2 by 37 in.

4.34 Abstract Couple.

4.36 AC 012 Abstract Couple, 1940, oil on linen, 40 by 68 in.

4.35 AC 007 Abstract Couple, 1955, oil on linen, 26 by 59 in.

Above Middle: 4.37 AC 010 Abstract Couple, 1940, oil on linen, 25 by 46 in.

Above: 4.38 AC 005 Abstract Couple, 1960, oil on canvas, 24 by 33 in.

Top: 4.39 AC 015 Abstract Couple, 1940, oil on linen, 21 1/2 by 44 1/2 in.

Middle: 4.40 AC 013 Abstract Couple, 1940, oil on linen, 29 by 29 in.

Bottom: 4.41 AC 014 Abstract Couple, 1940, oil on linen, 12 1/2 by 43 in.

Top: 4.42 AC 016 Abstract Couple, 1940, oil on linen, 35 by 47 1/2 in.

Bottom: 4.43 AC 008 Abstract Couple, 1960, oil on linen, 24 by 58 1/2 in.

Bottom: 4.44 AC 017 Abstract Couple, 1934, oil on linen, 20 by 28 in.

4.45 AC 018 Abstract Couple, 1980, oil on linen, 23 1/2 by 36 in.

4.46 AC 009 Abstract Couple, 1965, oil on linen, 35 by 49 in.

4.47 AC 020 Abstract Couple, 1928-32, oil on canvas, 27 1/2 by 39 in.

4.48 CO 001 Abstract Landscape, 1980, collage in oil, 11 1/2 by 14 in.

4.49 CO 004 Abstract Landscape, 1980, collage in oil, 12 by 12 in.

Above: 4.51 Abstract Landscape in purple, gold, and brown.

Top: 4.50 This and all of the following small studies of abstract landscapes were mounted in one of several binders that Sakier kept.

4.52 Abstract Landscape in light turquoise, earth tones, and black.

4.53 Abstract Landscape in clear turquoise, earth tones, and black.

4.54 Abstract Landscape in bright pinks, light green, and purple.

4.55 Abstract Landscape in magenta and black.

4.56 Abstract Landscape in neutral grays.

4.57 Abstract Landscape in neutral grays and browns.

4.58 Abstract Landscape in neutral grays and browns.

4.59 Abstract Landscape in neutrals and dull green.

4.60 Abstract Landscape in neutrals and gray-green.

4.61 Abstract Landscape in turquoise and earth tones.

4.62 Abstract Landscape in dark earth tones.

4.63 Abstract Landscape in neutrals.

4.64 Abstract Landscape in neutrals with dark green.

4.65 Abstract Landscape in earth tones.

4.66 Abstract Landscape in dull green and other earth tones.

4.67 Abstract Landscape in slate gray and other neutrals.

4.68 Abstract Landscape in gold, magenta, and neutrals.

4.69 Abstract Landscape in earth tones.

4.70 Abstract Landscape in neutrals with magenta accent.

4.71 Abstract Landscape in earth tones, dark purple, and magenta.

4.72 Abstract Landscape in earth tones with pink sky.

4.73 Abstract Landscape in dull pink and earth tones.

4.74 Abstract Landscape in light grays and pinks.

4.75 Abstract Landscape in blue-greens and grays with a touch of pink.

4.76 Abstract Landscape in cobalt, lavender-pink, and neutrals.

4.77 Abstract Landscape in cobalt, magenta, and neutrals.

4.78 Abstract Landscape in blue-purple and earth tones.

4.79 Abstract Landscape in burnt apricot and neutrals.

4.80 Abstract Landscape in earth tones and black

4.81 Abstract Landscape in pumpkin and earth tones.

4.82 Sakier in his Paris studio, 1982.

4.83 AC 003 Abstract Couple, oil on linen, 30 by 36 in., pictured on the easel in Sakier's studio.

4.84 View of Sakier's fireplace with Abstract Couple paintings, 1982

4.85 This and the following are examples of untitled and undated paintings. Although they are similar to some of the previous examples, the introduction of different shapes and colors is of interest.

4.86 Abstraction with blue egg.

4.87 Abstract Couples against moonlight.

4.88 Abstract Couple.

4.89 Abstract Seascape with black sea.

4.90 Abstract canoes.

4.91 Abstraction in red and pink.

4.92 Abstract Landscape in red and pink.

4.93 Abstract Landscape with red mountains at night.

4.94 Abstraction with reversed reflection.

4.95 Abstract couple with third party.

4.96 Abstract Landscape with pink sun.

Conclusion

Sakier devoted forty years of his life to painting. Investments from industrial design and Fostoria glass royalties insured that he did not need to sell his paintings to earn a living. Many were given to friends and family (unfortunately he had no children from his one marriage). In addition to the decades spent almost exclusively on painting, Sakier had also painted while actively designing for industry, so there is no way of estimating how many of his paintings are in New York, France, or elsewhere.

The Fostoria Glass Company produced more than one thousand different patterns and decorations during its century-long history. Sakier was a major, if not the main, consultant designer for more than half of that history. There is no telling how many designs he was responsible for — fully, partly, or as an influence on other designers. What remains of the company's records does not mention designers.

Only some of Sakier's glass or industrial designs were patented. Since only his most popular bathroom fixtures were mentioned or illustrated in contemporary literature, the exact number of his industrial designs is not known either. However, since he left the field and the country rather abruptly in about 1950, the number of these designs was more limited than the glass.

The dates of published articles and exhibits that included Sakier's industrial and glass designs coincided with the most important years of his career — from 1929 to 1951. He is not mentioned in print again (that I am aware of) until the mid 1970s — a gap that exceeded the length of his career and period of recognition. Martin Greif mentions Sakier in a 1975 publication, Jeffrey Meikle in 1979, and Karen Davies and Arthur Pulos in books published in 1983. He was acknowledged as being one of a group of pioneering American designers active in the late 1920s and 1930s.

While Sakier's glass designs have been presented in an industrial design context, books specifically about glass do not include his work. Eason Eige, however, acknowledged him as the designer of some Fostoria glass in a 1980 exhibition catalog; articles by Jon Saffell in a club newsletter in 1983 and by Barbara Adt in a newspaper for buying and selling Depression era glassware in 1986 were among the first to point out some of his Fostoria designs. Ironically, the publication that attracted the most attention was Christie's auction catalog for the Robert Mapplethorpe estate sale in New York in 1989, one year after Sakier had died. The price estimates and prices realized for molded Fostoria glass were shocking. This sudden jump in value was attributed to its designer, George Sakier.

In 1994 Pratt Institute held an exhibit of Sakier's paintings, along with a sample of glass designs, at its exhibition galleries in Manhattan and in Brooklyn and later published an exhibition catalog. Now that Sakier is no longer here to answer the many lingering questions, after a forty-year sleep, interest in his work has been awakened in the United States. Perhaps this book will contribute to arousing it further.

Notes

Chapter One

1. In a handwritten letter in the George Sakier Foundation archives (GSF Archives) dated Oct. 22, 1982, Sakier wrote, "In not one of my activities did I have any instruction beyond high school. I had six months of Columbia to get the necessary academic credits so as to take the post-graduate scholarship offered me. Got bored and quit."
2. As a result of his generator in 1917, Sakier's weekly salary went from $25 to $50.
3. According to a letter from editor Charles Hanson Towne, dated March 27, 1930, Sakier was director from June 1, 1929, to March 1, 1930. Actually, no two sources agree on the dates of Sakier's three art directorships.

Chapter Two

1. Cheney, Sheldon and Martha Chandler, *Art and the Machine* (New York: Whittlesey House, 1936), p. 80. This book is a classic with a very positive view of industrial design.
2. "Both Fish and Fowl," *Fortune* 9 (Feb. 1934), p. 97.
3. "Primer of Modern Design," *Arts and Decoration* 40 (Nov. 1933), p. 36.
4. Harry V. Anderson, "Contemporary American Designers," *The Decorators Digest* (July 1933), p. 39.
5. Rosemarie Haag Bletter in *High Styles: Twentieth-Century American Design*, (New York: Whitney Museum, 1985), p.109.
6. Ibid., p. 109.
7. Letter from David B. Dalzell to Sakier dated March 22, 1979, in GSF archives.
8. Letter from David B. Dalzell to Sakier dated March 22, 1981, in GSF archives.
9. Ann Kerr, *Fostoria*, (Paducah, Kentucky: Collector, 1994), p. 11; letter to the author Jan. 1995.

Chapter Three

1. "Both Fish and Fowl," p. 43.
2. Cheney, p. 215.
3. Ibid., pp. 41 & 46.
4. Ibid., p. 39.
5. Ibid., p. 44.
6. Greif, Martin, *Depression Modern* (New York: Universe, 1975), p. 35.
7. Meikle, Jeffrey, *Twentieth Century Limited* (Philadelphia: Temple U., 1979), p. 27.
8. Greif, p. 31; "Ten Years From Today — maybe," *Arts and Decoration* (Jan. 1935), p. 20.
9. Letter in GSF archives; "Fashions of the Future," *Vogue* 93 (Feb. 1, 1939), p. 144.
10. George Sakier, "Hot and Cold," photocopy of undated article in GSF archives.
11. "Plumbing by Mr. Sakier," *Arts and Decoration* 42 (March 1935), p.43.
12. Cheney, p. 79.
13. Harold Van Doren, *Industrial Design: A Practical Guide* (New York: McGraw-Hill, 1940), pp. xvii and 3.
14 "Both Fish and Fowl," p. 97.
15. "Modern Classic Design is More Than a Passing Style," *Crockery and Glass Journal* (Dec. 1933), p. 42.
16. Ibid., p. 43.
17. Cheney, pp. 186, 31, & 38.
18. Letter from former American Standard president, written from Palm Springs, California, to Sakier, dated March 15, 1951; according to a handwritten note on a copy of Sakier's résumé in the GSF archives, the annual salary went from $10,000 to $20,000; quotes from "What Others Say" page in the "Neo Classic" promotional brochure.
19. "Both Fish and Fowl," p. 97.
20. See, for example, *The Studio Yearbook*, (1936), pp. 120 & 121; George Sakier, "New ideas for bathroom and kitchen," *House & Garden* 62 (Aug. 1932), p. 36.
21 Anderson, p. 40;"Ten Years From Today," p. 20.
22. "Both Fish and Fowl," p. 98; Cheney, p. 79.
23. *House Furnishing Review* (May 1933), p. 28.
24. George Sakier, "Her Kitchen," *House & Garden* 70 (Oct. 1936), pp. 142, 143, & 158; "New ideas for bathroom and kitchen," p. 37.
25. Richardson Wright, "Husbands in Interior Decoration," *House & Garden* (Feb. 1928).
26. George Sakier, "Rooms in Black, White, and Gray," *House & Garden* 56 (Sept. 1929); "Permanent floor coverings — a review," *House & Garden* 67 (Feb. 1935).
27. "Ten Years From Today," pp. 20-21.
28. *Studio Yearbook* 1935, p. 74.
29. Cheney, p. 78.
30. Letter from Schenley Products executive, Grover A. Whalen, dated Sept. 18, 1934, in GSF archives.
31. Letter in GSF archives; Society of Industrial Designers, *51 U. S. Industrial Design*, (New York: Studio Publications, 1951), p. 154.
32. The following information regarding Sakier's part in the fair was taken from a typescript of World's Fair press release prepared by the Department of Feature Publicity, with a release date of May 26, 1939, in GSF archives.
33. Ibid., p. 3.
34. Ibid., p. 5.
35. "The latest bath news from the World's Fair" photocopy in GSF archives.
36. Arthur Pulos, *American Design Ethic* (Cambridge: MIT Press, 1983), p. 402; Pulos, *The American Design Adventure* (Cambridge: MIT Press, 1988), p. 200.
37. Quoted in *American Design Adventure*, p. 200.
38. *American Design Adventure*, p. 200.
39. Ibid., p. 176; Van Doren, p. 78.
40. *American Design Ethic*, p. 422.

Chapter Four

1. "Sakier" exhibition brochure, Parrish Art Museum, 1970 in GSF Archives.
2. Ibid; "George Sakier on His Work," photocopy in GSF Archives.
3. "Sakier."
4. Ross Neher, "George Sakier: Correspondences," Pratt Institute exhibit, 1994.
5. letter from Sakier to Raoul Schrott dated 1987, in GSF Archives.
6. "Sakier."
7. Ibid.
8. Neher.
9 "Sakier."
10. Sakier numbered paintings rather than title them. The abbreviation RL = Realistic Landscape; AL = Abstract Landscape; RC = Realistic Couple; AC = Abstract Couple; CO = Abstract Collage; M = Still Life.

Select Bibliography

All of the following sources include material about Sakier and/or illustrate his work.

Adt, Barbara. "Somewhere In Time...George Sakier Designer, Fostoria Glass Co." *The Daze* (Feb. 1986): 43.

———. "From Renaissance to Fostoria." *Facets of Fostoria* (Dec. 1992): 5-7.

Anderson, Harry V. "Contemporary American Designers." *The Decorators Digest* (July 1933): 38-41.

Architectural League of New York. *Year Book of the Architectural League of New: Catalogue of the Forty-Eighth Annual Exhibition.* New York: Kalkhoff Press, 1933.

"Art and Machine." *The Architectural Forum.* (May 1934): 334-35.

"Both Fish and Fowl." *Fortune.* 9 (Feb. 1934): 40-43, 80, 90-98.

Byars, Mel. "George Sakier." *The Design Encyclopedia.* New York: John Wiley & Sons, 1994.

Byars, Mel and Russel Flinchum, eds. *50 American Designers.* (Washington: Preservation Press, 1994).

Cheney, Sheldon and Martha Chandler. *Art and the Machine: An Account of Industrial Design in 20th-century America.* New York: Whittlesey House, 1936.

Christie's. *The Collection of Robert Mapplethorpe.* New York (Oct. 31, 1989): lots 106-109.

Clark, Juliet and Florence. "Decorative Value of Modern Table Glass." *Arts and Decoration* 34 (April 1931): 34-35.

"Classic Themes." *Arts and Decoration* 40 (April 1934): 44.

Corning Museum of Glass. *Glass 1959.* Corning, New York: Corning Museum, 1959.

Country Life 64 (Sept. 1933): 37. untitled article.

"Contemporary American Glass." Unknown author, source, date.

"Credo of an Industrial Designer." Unknown author, source, date.

Davies, Karen. *At Home in Manhattan: Modern Decorative Arts 1925 to the Depression.* New Haven: Yale U. Press, 1983.

Duncan, Alastair. *American Art Deco.* New York: Harry N. Abrams, 1986.

Eige, Eason. *A Century of Glassmaking in West Virginia.* Huntington, West Virginia: Huntington Galleries, 1980.

Elegant American Glassware of the early 1900's. Hollywood, Florida Culture Center exhibition catalog, Sept. 6 - Oct. 14, 1983.

Falk, Peter Hastings ed. "George Sakier." *Who Was Who in American Art.* Madison, Connecticut: Sound View Press, 1985.

"Fashions of the Future." *Vogue* 93 (Feb. 1, 1939): 71-78 & 137-146.

Fostoria Glass Company. Records in manuscript collection of the Ohio Historical Center, Columbus, Ohio.

———. Trade catalogs in the microfiche collection of the Corning Museum of Glass, Corning, New York.

Gauthron, Bernard. "George Sakier a la Fondation Mona Bismarck." *La Cote des Arts* (Feb. 1987): 34.

"George Sakier: Artist and Machine Become Reconciled." Unknown author, source, or date. 46-47 & 66.

George Sakier Foundation. Archives: papers, photographs, letters, and other material written or collected by George Sakier, to be referred to as "GSF

Archives."
"George Sakier, Pioneer Industrial Designer, Exhibits." *Art Alliance Bulletin* (Nov. 1944): 5.
Greif, Martin. *Depression Modern: The Thirties Style in America.* New York: Universe, 1975.
Hanks, David A. and Jennifer Toher. *Donald Deskey: Decorative Designs and Interiors.* New York: E. P. Dutton, 1987.
"Industrial Arts Exhibit." *Architectural Forum* (May 1934): 334-35.
Israel, Judith. Niece of George Sakier. Personal interview Oct. 22, 1994.
Kerr, Ann. *Fostoria: An Identification and Value Guide.* Paducah, Kentucky: Collector Books, 1994.
"The latest bath news from the World's Fair." Unknown author or source; photocopy in GSF archives.
Litman, William and Lyla. "Fostoria No. 2412 Colony Pattern." Moundsville, WV: Fostoria Glass Society of America, 1990.
Long, Milbra and Emily Seate. "Jamestown Pattern No. 2719." 1992.
———. *Fostoria Stemware: The Crystal for America.* Paducah, Kentucky: Collector Books, 1994.
Marquis. "George Sakier." *Who's Who in America.* 38th edition 1974-75, Vol. 2. Chicago: Marquis Who's Who Inc., 1974.
Meikle, Jeffrey. *Twentieth-Century Limited.* Philadelphia: Temple U. Press, 1979.
Neher, Ross. "George Sakier: Correspondences." New York: Pratt Institute Exhibitions, 1994, printed sheet distributed at exhibit.
"Neo Classic." promotional brochure. Pittsburgh: Standard Sanitary Manufacturing Co., 1931.
"Notes on Glass Design." Unknown author, source, or date.
Parrish Art Museum. "Sakier." exhibition brochure. Southampton, New York: Parrish Art Museum, 1970.
Philadelphia Art Alliance. "George Sakier, Pioneer Industrial Designer Exhibits." *Art Alliance Bulletin.* (Nov. 1944): 5.
Pile, John. *The Dictionary of 20th Century Design.* New York: Da Capo Press, 1994.
Piña, Leslie. *Fostoria: Serving the American Table 1887-1986.* Atglen, Pennsylvania: Schiffer, 1995.
———. "George Sakier, American Designer 1897-1988." in Pratt Institute. exhibition catalog. *George Sakier.* Brooklyn: Pratt Institute, 1995.
"Plumbing by Mr. Sakier." *Arts and Decoration* 42 (March 1935): 42-43.
Pratt Institute. News releases and other papers related to Sakier exhibit, 1994.
———. *George Sakier.* Exhibition catalog. Brooklyn: Pratt Institute, 1995.
"Primer of Modern Design." *Arts and Decoration* 40 (Nov. 1933): 36-37.
Pulos, Arthur J. *American Design Ethic: A History of Industrial Design to 1940.* Cambridge: MIT Press, 1983.
———. *The American Design Adventure 1940-1975.* Cambridge: MIT Press, 1988.
Saffell, Jon. "Fostoria Glass Company's Design Dept. — A History." *Facets of Fostoria* 2 (Nos. 1-5 1983).
———. Personal interview. March 1994. Saffell was the last to head Fostoria's design department.
"Sakier: Artist-into-merchandiser." Unknown author, source, date.
"Sakier Designs a Dressing Table." *House Furnishing Review 78* (May 1933): 28.
Sakier, George. "Credo of an Industrial Designer." Unknown source or date.
———. "Her Kitchen." *House & Garden* 70 (Oct. 1936): 142-43, 158.
———. "Hot and Cold." Unknown source or date.
———. "Modern Classic Design Is More Than A Passing Style." *Crockery and Glass Journal* (Dec. 1933): 42-43.
———. "New Ideas For Bathroom and Kitchen." *House & Garden* 62 (Aug. 1932): 36-37.
———. "No Mechanistic Clothes for Future Women Predicts George Sakier." *Vogue* 93 (Feb. 1, 1939): 144.
———. "Permanent Floor Coverings — A Review." *House & Garden* 67 (Feb. 1935): 37 & 69.
———. "Rooms in Black, White and Gray." *House & Garden* 56 (Sept. 1929): 90, 140.
"Sakier Realist." Unknown author, source, date.
"Samuel Sakier" obituary. *New York Times* (Jan. 4, 1934): 19:2.
Schrott, Raoul. *Dada 21/22.* Insbruk, Austria: Haymon-Verlad, 1988.
"Seventeen Years of Industrial Design at the Metropolitan Museum of Art." *Arts and Decoration* 42 (Feb. 1935): 32-33.
Society of Industrial Designers. *U.S. Industrial Design 1949-1950.* New York: Studio Publications, 1949.
———. *51 U. S. Industrial Design.* New York: Studio Publications, 1951.
———. *Industrial Design in America, 1954.* New York: Farrar, Straus & Young, [1954].
Sotheby's. *Twentieth Century Decorative Arts.* New York, June 10 & 11, 1993, lot 62.

Sprackling, Helen. "The Glory of Glass." *Country Life* 64 (Sept. 1933): 35-37.

Storey, Walter Rendell. "Unification in Modern Design: George Sakier — Interior Decorator." *The Studio* 123 (March 1942): 66-69.

The Studio Yearbook of Decorative Art. London: The Studio Ltd, 1931, 1933, 1935, 1936, 1937 & 1939. Title may also be *Decorative Art,* or *The Studio,* or *Year Book of "The Studio."*

———. "Kitchen Designed by George Sakier." (1939): 55.

"Table Talk." *Arts and Decoration* 39 (Sept. 1933).

Teague, Walter. "The Cash Value of Design." *Arts and Decoration* 43 (Jan. 1936): 34-35, 48.

"Ten Years From Today — maybe." *Arts and Decoration* (Jan. 1935): 20-23.

United States Patent Office Records.

Van Doren, Harold. *Industrial Design: A Practical Guide.* New York: McGraw-Hill, 1940.

Weatherman, Hazel Marie. *Fostoria: Its First Fifty Years.* Springfield, Missouri: Weathermans, 1972.

Weber, Eva. *Art Deco In America.* New York: Exeter, 1985.

———. *American Art Deco.* New York: Crescent, 1992.

Whitney Museum of American Art. *High Styles: Twentieth-Century American Design.* New York: Whitney Museum, 1985.

Wilson, Richard Guy, Dianne Pilgrim, and Dickran Tashjian. *The Machine Age In America 1918-1941.* New York: Harry N. Abrams, 1986.

Wright, Richardson. "Husbands in Interior Decoration." *House and Garden* 55 (Feb. 1929).

Appendix: Pattern List

Sakier Designs for Fostoria Glass

892 Nordic, 1939
1372 Coin shapes
2387 vase
2402 geometric bowl and candleholders
2404 vase
2408 vase
2409 vase
2412 Colony stems, pickle dish, plate, and others, 1939
2419 Mayfair, 1930
2425 bowl, vase, candles
2427 cigarette box with cover
2428 Lotus vases
2430 Diadem, 1929 matching 6202 (6002) stems 1930
2447 duo candlestick
2453 candlestick, 1931
2484 and 2496 Baroque candlesticks, candelabra, handled bowl, vase, etc., 1934
2510 Sunray candlesticks, 1935, probably more in pattern
2527 candle, 1936
2545 Flame candleholders, vase, tray
2550 Spool, 1938
2560 Coronet plates and others, 1938
2563 Viking bowl and candlestick, 1939
2592 Myriad vases and bowls, 1940s
2594 plume candlesticks, bowl
2636 Plume candlesticks, bookend, 1950
2638 s-scroll candlestick
2639 ivy duo candlestick, bowl, 1950
2652 candlestick
2667 candlestick
2668 candlestick
2718 Fairmont, 1958
2719 Jamestown, 1958
2731 cigarette box
2746 pressed Chinese ashtray
2747 ashtray
2748 ashtray
2749 Windsor crown, late 1950s
2750 Hapsburg crown, late 1950s
2751 Navarre crown, late 1950s
2760 including 5 1/2-in. candlestick
2761 candlestick
2762 candlestick
2763 candlestick, also used with chimney
2764 candlestick
2765 candlestick
2766 Luxembourg crown
2767 candlestick
2832 Sorrento, 1972
4020 crystal stems, bud vase
4120 ebony base or color stems, 1929, decanter, cream & sugar
4021 and 4121 finger bowl, 1929
4024 Victorian stems, 1933
5650 Horizon, 1952, plus barware
6011 Classic stems and Whirlpool 730 cutting
6012 Westchester stems, 1936
6017 Sceptre stems, 1938
6019 Rondel stems, 1938
6020 Melody stems
6023 candlestick
6027 Envoy stems, 1940
6030 Astrid stems, 1942

6031 stem
6033 Mademoiselle stems, 1949
6037 Silver Flutes stems, 1949
6044 Tiara 1951
6045 Capri
6064 Patrician, 1956
6064 1/2 Elegance ribbed optic
6113 Versailles blown crystal stemware with 683 gold decoration on stem, 1969

Possible Sakier Designs

2364 Sonata
2390 bowl
2395 1/2 spiral candle and bowl
2433 Grecian bowls and candlesticks
2467 Neo classical vase
2472 candlestick
2482 candlestick
2533 candlestick
2538 placecard holder
2546 quadrangle candlestick and bowls
2601 Lyre candlestick, bookend, and bowl
2619 vase
2638/2666 Contour
2640 garden & candle
2652 candlestick
2653 candlestick
2655 candlestick
2670 Dawn, 1960
2671 Dusk, 1960
2685 Seascape
2720, 2726-2730 Heirloom
2737 Hawaiian
2739 Roulette
2740-2745 Sculpture
4161 Karnak
4183 Homespun
6020 stem
6023 Colfax stem, 1940
6024 Celini stem, 1940
6025 stem
6036 Rutledge
6055 Marilyn

PRICE GUIDE

Although most price ranges listed in this guide reflect typical asking and selling prices for Fostoria items across the country, some take into account the added significance of being designed by George Sakier. It is therefore possible that this guide will become obsolete sooner than others. Only the buyers and sellers can determine this. If collectors value Sakier Fostoria glass more highly than other Fostoria, the prices will reflect it. Common/popular Sakier patterns, such as Colony and Jamestown, and late patterns, such as Sorrento, may not be as sensitive to price changes (increases) as are the more important, early, or rare designs: 4020 and 6202 stems; Art Deco 2402, 2404, 2408, 2409, and 2428; Myriad, Diadem, Spool, Viking, Baroque, Flame, and other modern designs. These and other outstanding examples of American modernism transcend Fostoria and will undoubtedly be looked at more seriously by both collectors of Fostoria and of modernism.

Where most Fostoria collectors prefer their stems etched, their candleholders with bobeches and prisms, and colors in the blue to lavender end of the spectrum, collectors of Sakier glass have other criteria. Form was foremost to Sakier, and contemporary photographs display plain candleholders as he designed them. Surface decorations, if any, were simple and modern — Whirlpool, Comet, Manhattan, Polka Dot; ebony and crystal were often more effective than color. Only in company catalogs do we find distracting prisms dripping from candlesticks or traditional etchings oddly smothering clean forms.

With this in mind, the user of this guide is encouraged to consult it gently. Obviously, the publisher cannot be responsible for any transaction outcomes, but hopes that this book can give you a bit of an edge... for awhile.

All pieces are assumed to be in perfect condition. Prices are in U. S. dollars. The following position code is used: L=left; R=right; T=top; B=bottom; C=center; TL=top left; TR=top right; CL=center left; CR=center right.

page	photo	position	price
15	2.1		30-40
	2.2	L	150-200
		R	30-40
16	2.3		15-20 each
17	2.5		200-400 each
18	2.6	L	200-250
		R	100-150
	2.7		100-200 each
19	2.8	L	75-100
		C	80-120
		R	40-60
20	2.10		30-40 each
	2.11		30-40 each
22	2.16		200-300
	2.17		200-250
23	2.18		200-400 each
24	2.19		200-400 each
25	2.20		200-400 each
	2.21		200-400 each
26	2.22		150-250
	2.23		150-250
27	2.24		150-250
	2.25		150-250
	2.26		150-250
28	2.27	T	100-150
		B	25-35
	2.28	T	100—150
		B	25-35 each
	2.29	T	100-150
		B	25-35 each
29	2.30		25-35 each
	2.31	T	60-90 each
		B	25-35 each
	2.32		30-50 each
31	2.37		30-40 each
	2.39		30-40 each
32	2.40		30-40 each
	2.42		30-40
33	2.43		30-40 each

	2.44		30-40 each
	2.45		30-40 each
34	2.46		30-40 each
	2.47		30-40 each
	2.48		60-80 set
35	2.49		30-35 each
	2.50		30-35 each
36	2.53		30-35
37	2.54		40-60 each
38	2.57	L	100-200
		R	30-40
	2.58		30-40 each
39	2.59		50-75 each
40	2.61		45-65
	2.62	T	10-15
		B	15-20 set
41	2.64		25-35
	2.65		10-15 each
	2.66		10-20 each
42	2.67	L	15-25
		R	20-30
	2.68		15-25 each
			30-40 wisteria
43	2.69		80-120 pair
	2.70		80-120 pair
	2.71		80-120 pair
44	2.72		50-75
	2.74		100-175 pair
45	2.75		50-75
	2.77		20-25 each
	2.78		30-40
46	2.79		75-150 pair
47	2.82		50-100 pair
	2.83		40-80 pair
	2.84		20-40
48	2.85		100-200 pair
49	2.87		150-250 pair
50	2.89		150-250 pair
	2.91		100-200 pair
51	2.92		60-90 pair
	2.94		80-120 pair
52	2.95		25-40 each
	2.97		60-90
53	2.98		50-75
54	2.101		60-90
55	2.103		75-100 each
56	2.105	C	75-100 each

		L & R	75-100 pair
	2.106		75-105 pair
	2.107		75-100 pair
	2.108		100-150 pair
57	2.109		20-25 each
	2.110		20-25 each
58	2.111		20-25 each
59	2.114		30-40 each
60	2.117		20-30 each
	2.118		20-30 each
	2.119		20-25 each
61	2.120		20-30 each
62	2.123		20-25 each
	2.124		20-25 each
63	2.125		20-25 each
64	2.128		30-50
	2.129		100-150
	2.130		80-120
65	2.131		20-25
	2.132		200-250 pair
	2.133		75-100
66	2.134		80-120 pair
	2.135		60-90
	2.136		100-150 pair
68	2.138		100-150 pair
69	2.140		30-40 set
	2.143		15-20 each
70	2.144		20-25 each
	2.146		20-25 each
71	2.147	L	20-30
		CL	20-25
		CR	20-25
		R	20-25
74	2.154		10-15 each
	2.155		15-20 each
	2.156		15-20 each
	2.157	TC	30-40
		L & R	15-20 each
75	2.158		30-40
77	2.163		60-90 pair
78	2.165		60-90
	2.167		15-20 each
79	2.168	T	75-100
		BR	15-20
	2.169		100-150 pair
	2.170		20-30
80	2.171		20-25 each

	2.172		20-25 each
	2.173		20-25 each
85	2.183		75-100 each
	2.184		60-90
86	2.186		10-20 each
	2.188		10-20 each
87	2.189		10-20 each
	2.190		10-20 each
88	2.192		10-20 each
			set
	2.194		10-15 each
89	2.195		20-30
	2.196		20-30
	2.197		20-30
90	2.199		15-25 each
91	2.201		20-30 each
	2.202		20-30
92	2.203		15-20 each
93	2.205		15-20
	2.206		20-30
	2.207		20-30
94	2.208		10-20 each
	2.209	L	10-15
		C	15-25
		R	15-20
95	2.210		75-150 each
96	2.211	L	80-100
		C	30-45
		R	60-80
	2.212	L	60-90
		C	40-60
		R	40-60
97	2.213	L	30-50
		C	60-90
		R	15-25
	2.214		100-150
	2.215		40-60
98	2.216		150-250 pair
	2.217		50-75
	2.218		30-40 each
99	2.219		10-20 each
100	2.222		10-20 each
	2.223		10-20 each
	2.224		10-15 each
	2.225		10-15 each
101	2.226		10-15
	2.227		10-15 each

Index

L

M

N

P

R

S

T

U

V

W